Better Homes and Gardens®

TOASTEROVEN
COOK BOOK

© 1982 by Meredith Corporation, Des Moines, Iowa.
All Rights Reserved. Printed in the United States of America.
First Edition. Third Printing, 1983.
Library of Congress Catalog Card Number: 81-67154
ISBN: 0-696-00785-1

On the cover:
Vegetable-Brat Kabobs (see recipe, page 76)
Individual Cheesecakes (see recipe, page 86)

BETTER HOMES AND GARDENS® BOOKS
Editor: Gerald M. Knox
Art Director: Ernest Shelton
Managing Editor: David A. Kirchner

Food and Nutrition Editor: Doris Eby
Department Head—Cook Books: Sharyl Heiken
Senior Food Editor: Elizabeth Woolever
Senior Associate Food Editors: Sandra Granseth, Rosemary C.
    Hutchinson
Associate Food Editors: Jill Burmeister, Julia Martinusen, Diana
    McMillen, Marcia Stanley, Diane Yanney
Recipe Development Editor: Marion Viall
Test Kitchen Director: Sharon Stilwell
Test Kitchen Home Economists: Jean Brekke, Kay Cargill, Marilyn
    Cornelius, Maryellyn Krantz, Marge Steenson

Associate Art Director (Managing): Randall Yontz
Associate Art Directors (Creative): Linda Ford, Neoma Alt West
Copy and Production Editors: Nancy Nowiszewski, Lamont Olson,
    Mary Helen Schiltz, David A. Walsh
Assistant Art Directors: Faith Berven, Harijs Priekulis
Graphic Designers: Mike Burns, Alisann Dixon, Mike Eagleton,
    Lynda Haupert, Deb Miner, Lyne Neymeyer, Bill Shaw,
    D. Greg Thompson

Editor in Chief: Neil Kuehnl
Group Editorial Services Director: Duane L. Gregg
Executive Art Director: William J. Yates

General Manager: Fred Stines
Director of Publishing: Robert B. Nelson
Director of Retail Marketing: Jamie Martin
Director of Direct Marketing: Arthur Heydendael

TOASTER OVEN COOK BOOK
Editor: Diane Yanney
Copy and Production Editor: Lamont Olson
Graphic Designer: Bill Shaw

Our seal assures you that every recipe in the *Toaster Oven Cook Book* is endorsed by the Better Homes and Gardens Test Kitchen. Each recipe is tested for family appeal, practicality, and deliciousness.

CONTENTS

INTRODUCTION

If you think a toaster oven is only good for baking potatoes, reheating pizza, and making toast, then you are shortchanging this handy appliance. Although smaller than a conventional oven, a toaster oven is capable of baking and broiling many of your favorite foods—just in small quantities. That's what this cook book is all about: small quantities. It's a collection of recipes sized especially for the toaster oven so you won't have to heat up your large oven to bake a small casserole or a few cookies, or to prepare a broiled vegetable. Chapters are organized so you can choose recipes that fit your oven's capabilities—whether they be toasting, baking, and/or broiling. Don't overlook the menu section featuring recipes for complete meals for one or two, including salads, side dishes, and desserts.

Like any other appliance, the toaster oven will be most useful if you take time to become acquainted with its features. Because models vary, it is important that you read the manufacturer's instructions. Take special note of preheating directions and recommended baking utensils.

Once you become familiar with how your toaster oven works "on paper," you will need to learn how it performs. Before attempting anything exotic, broil or bake some simple foods. A pork chop works well for a broiling test. You'll be able to see how evenly the meat is broiled and how the closeness of the broiling pan to the heating element affects cooking time. Note any major differences in cook-ing time between your oven and the time suggested in the chart on page 65 so you'll remember to adjust each accordingly.

To learn how your oven browns, bake a package of refrigerated biscuits. If top browning is uneven, you may have to turn the biscuits or baking tray halfway through the cooking time. If food has browned too much on the bottom, use an oven thermometer to check the accuracy of your temperature control. Again, note any adjustments for future recipes.

When adapting your own recipes, keep in mind the oven's limited capacity. Use baking pans small enough to allow heat to circulate. Remember that the finished height of baked foods cannot exceed the pan height recommended by the appliance manufacturer.

For heating or reheating foods in the toaster oven, use the chart below as a helpful guide.

HEATING/REHEATING FOODS

FOOD	TEMP.	TIME (minutes)
Baking Potatoes	425°	40 to 50
Baking Chicken Pieces	350°	about 45
Baking Pork Chops (½ inch)	350°	about 45
Warming Sandwiches	350°	about 25
Heating Frozen Pizza	425°	12 to 15
Heating Frozen Meat Pies	425°	30 to 35
Reheating Bread/Rolls	350°	about 3
Reheating Leftovers (1 cup) Place in individual casserole or wrap in foil	350°	10 to 15
Reheating Chilled Pizza	400°	about 5
Crisping Crackers/Cookies Spread in single layer on baking tray	350°	2 to 3

Note: To heat frozen dinner entrées, follow package directions.

Do you wonder whether you have the right size baking equipment for toaster oven recipes? To check your utensils, use these easy methods. For recipes that specify pan dimensions, use a ruler to measure pans from one inside edge to the opposite inside edge for both width and length. Then measure the height of the pan along an inside edge.

For volume capacities (1-quart, 15-ounces, etc.), use a liquid measuring cup to fill baking pans with water to the top. Keep track of how much water is used to fill the utensil. The amount used is the capacity.

But measuring is not always enough. Decorative casseroles may not fit into your oven if they have handles. Set baking dishes on the baking tray before preparing any recipe. Then you'll know whether your pans fit.

TOASTING

These toast toppers will brighten breakfasts or snacks. Simply spread them on bread, bagels, English muffins, frozen French toast, or waffles. Then toast the bread and topper all at once. From lower right to left are *Ham and Cheese Topper*, *Smoky Sausage Spread*, *Seafood Spread*, and *Herb-Cheese Spread* (see recipes, page 8).

In this chapter, you'll also find dessert recipes for toppers made to spread or sprinkle on angel cake, pound cake, brown bread, or nut bread slices.

TOASTING BREAD SPREADS

Ham and Cheese Topper

Pictured on pages 6 and 7—

2 6¾-ounce cans chunk-style ham, drained and flaked
1 cup shredded cheddar cheese (4 ounces)
1 teaspoon prepared mustard
½ teaspoon caraway seed
2 to 3 tablespoons mayonnaise

Combine first four ingredients. Stir in enough mayonnaise to make of spreading consistency. Spread on bread, bagels, or English muffins. Place on rack in oven. Toast at medium setting. Store in refrigerator. Makes 1½ cups.

To Freeze: Pack in juice can or baking pan (see tip, page 9).

Smoky Sausage Spread

Pictured on pages 6 and 7—

½ of a 12-ounce package fully cooked smoked sausage links
1 8-ounce jar cheese spread with jalapeño peppers
1 cup shredded Monterey Jack cheese (4 ounces)

Finely chop sausage; set aside. Combine cheese spread and Monterey Jack cheese; beat with electric mixer till well combined. Stir in sausage. Spread on bread, bagels, or English muffins. Toast at medium setting. Store in refrigerator. Makes about 2 cups.

To Freeze: Spread in baking pan (see tip, page 9).

Seafood Spread

Pictured on pages 6 and 7—

1 cup shredded Swiss cheese
½ cup dairy sour cream
1 tablespoon butter
1 6-ounce can crab meat, drained, flaked, and cartilage removed
1 4½-ounce can shrimp, rinsed, drained, and finely chopped
1 tablespoon thinly sliced green onion
1 teaspoon lemon juice

Combine cheese, sour cream, and butter; beat till fluffy. Stir in remaining ingredients. Spread on bread, bagels, or English muffins. Place on rack in oven. Toast at medium setting. Store in refrigerator. Makes 2¼ cups.

To Freeze: Spread in baking pan (see tip, page 9).

Herb-Cheese Spread

Pictured on pages 6 and 7—

2 cups shredded mozzarella cheese (8 ounces)
1 6- or 8-ounce container Neufchâtel cheese spread with onion
1 tablespoon dried parsley flakes
½ teaspoon dried savory, crushed
½ cup shelled sunflower nuts

Combine cheeses, parsley, and savory; beat with electric mixer till fluffy. Stir in nuts. Spread on bread, bagels, or English muffins. Toast at medium setting. Store in refrigerator. Makes 2¼ cups.

To Freeze: Pack in juice can or spread in baking pan (see tip, page 9).

CUTTING FROZEN BREAD TOPPERS

To make handy round slices, first pack the topper mixture into empty 6-ounce juice cans. Cover and freeze. At serving time, open the bottom of the can with a can opener. Push on the loosened bottom to push the frozen mixture out the other end. Slice off the desired amount of topper.

To make topper squares, spread the topper mixture into a 9x9x2-inch baking pan. Freeze the mixture till firm. Cut the frozen mixture into 16 squares. Wrap each square in moisture-vaporproof wrap. Store in freezer.

Store assorted bread toppers in the freezer for quick snacks and easy breakfasts. Pack the topper mixture into empty 6-ounce juice cans with tops removed. Cover cans with moisture-vaporproof wrap and freeze. To serve, open the bottom of the can with a can opener. Use loosened bottom to push spread out of can. Slice the desired amount of spread and return the remaining spread to the freezer.

For spreads that will not slice easily, turn the mixture into a 9x9x2-inch baking pan and freeze about 3 hours or till firm. Cut into 16 squares. Wrap each square in moisture-vaporproof wrap and store in the freezer. To serve the spreads, place a frozen slice or square atop toasted bread, bagel, or English muffin. Bake in a 350° oven about 5 minutes or till the topper is heated through.

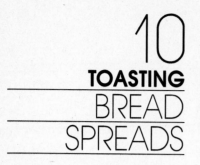

Peanut Butter Topper

1 cup peanut butter
1 3-ounce package cream
   cheese, softened
½ cup milk
2 tablespoons honey
½ cup raisins, chopped, *or*
   pitted dates, finely
   snipped
¼ cup finely chopped pecans

In a mixing bowl stir together peanut butter and cream cheese; gradually stir in milk and honey. Stir in raisins or dates and pecans. Spread on bread, bagels, or English muffins. Toast at medium setting. Store in refrigerator. Makes about 2¼ cups.

To Freeze: Spread in baking pan (see tip, page 9).

Cheesy Vegetable Spread

2 cups shredded mozzarella
   cheese (8 ounces)
¼ cup mayonnaise *or* salad
   dressing
½ teaspoon Italian seasoning
½ cup shredded carrot
3 tablespoons thinly sliced
   green onion
2 tablespoons finely chopped
   pimiento

In a mixing bowl combine the mozzarella cheese, mayonnaise or salad dressing, and Italian seasoning; mix well. Stir in the carrot, onion, and pimiento. Spread on bread, bagels, or English muffins. Toast at medium setting. Store in refrigerator. Makes about 2 cups.

To Store: Pack in juice can or baking pan (see tip, page 9).

Fruity Toast Topper

1 8¼-ounce can crushed
   pineapple, drained
1 8-ounce package cream
   cheese, softened
¼ cup cranberry-orange
   relish
½ teaspoon ground cinnamon

In a bowl combine crushed pineapple, cream cheese, cranberry-orange relish, and cinnamon. Spread on bread, bagels, or English muffins. Toast at medium setting. Store in refrigerator. Makes 1¾ cups.

To Freeze: Spread in baking pan (see tip, page 9).

Dilled Tuna Topper

1 3¼-ounce can tuna,
   drained and flaked
½ cup shredded American
   cheese (2 ounces)
½ cup shredded Monterey
   Jack cheese (2 ounces)
2 tablespoons finely chopped
   walnuts
2 tablespoons mayonnaise *or*
   salad dressing
1 teaspoon lemon juice
½ teaspoon dried parsley
   flakes
¼ teaspoon dried dillweed

In a mixing bowl combine tuna, American cheese, Monterey Jack cheese, walnuts, mayonnaise or salad dressing, lemon juice, parsley, and dillweed. Mix well. Spread on bread, bagels, or English muffins. Toast at medium setting. Store in refrigerator. Makes 2 cups.

To Freeze: Spread in baking pan (see tip, page 9).

TOASTING
DESSERTS

French Toast S'mores

4 slices frozen French toast
2 1.05-ounce bars milk chocolate, broken into squares
1 cup tiny marshmallows
2 tablespoons slivered almonds (optional)

Place French toast on rack in oven. Toast at medium setting. Arrange chocolate squares atop toast; sprinkle with marshmallows and nuts. Toast at light setting or till toast is heated through and marshmallows are golden brown. Makes 4 servings.

Doughnut Sundaes

2 unfrosted plain doughnuts
1 tablespoon butter, softened
2 teaspoons sugar
¼ teaspoon ground cinnamon
Coffee-flavored ice cream
Dark crème de cacao *or* chocolate-flavored syrup
Chopped nuts, coconut, *or* chocolate-flavored sprinkles

Slice doughnuts in half horizontally. Spread each cut side with butter. Combine sugar and cinnamon; sprinkle atop buttered sides. Place doughnuts cut side up, on rack in oven. Toast at light setting till cinnamon-sugar topping is crispy. Top each doughnut half with a scoop of ice cream. Drizzle with crème de cacao or chocolate syrup. Sprinkle with nuts, coconut, or sprinkles. Serves 4.

Peanut Revel Cake

¼ cup chunky-style *or* creamy peanut butter
2 tablespoons marshmallow creme
4 ½-inch-thick slices angel cake
¼ cup semisweet chocolate pieces *or* butterscotch pieces

Combine peanut butter and marshmallow creme. Spread *each* cake slice with *1 tablespoon* peanut butter mixture. Sprinkle top of *each* cake slice with *1 tablespoon* chocolate or butterscotch pieces. Place slices on rack in oven. Toast at medium setting till chocolate pieces melt and topping is bubbly. Makes 4 servings.

Toasted Cherry-Cheese-Topped Cake

½ loaf frozen pound cake, thawed
½ of a 4-ounce container whipped cream cheese
2 tablespoons finely chopped pecans
2 teaspoons milk
⅛ teaspoon ground cinnamon
2 tablespoons cherry *or* raspberry preserves

Cut cake into 4 slices. Combine cream cheese, pecans, milk, and cinnamon. Spread ¼ of the mixture on 1 side of each cake slice. Spoon ¼ of the preserves atop each. Place slices, topping side up, on rack in oven. Toast at medium setting. Makes 4 servings.

Brown Bread Shortcakes

1 beaten egg
3 tablespoons lemon juice
⅓ cup sugar
2 tablespoons butter *or* margarine, cut up
1 16-ounce can brown bread
1 4-ounce container whipped cream cheese
1 tablespoon sugar
¼ teaspoon ground cinnamon
¼ teaspoon vanilla
Dash ground nutmeg
Assorted fresh fruits

For lemon sauce, in small saucepan combine egg, lemon juice, the ⅓ cup sugar, and butter or margarine. Cook over medium-low heat, stirring constantly, (about 5 minutes) till mixture is thickened and bubbly. Cover and chill till serving time.

Cut brown bread into ten ½-inch slices. Combine cream cheese, the 1 tablespoon sugar, cinnamon, vanilla, and nutmeg. Spread about 1½ tablespoons on a bread slice. Top with another bread slice. Repeat with remaining bread slices and cream cheese mixture to make 5 shortcake stacks. Place brown bread stacks on rack in oven. Toast at medium setting till shortcakes are warm. Place on serving plates. Slice or cut up fruits as needed; spoon atop short-cakes. Drizzle lemon sauce over shortcakes. Makes 5 servings.

Cherry-Topped Waffles

Try this topper on toasted pound cake or angel cake slices—

8 frozen waffles
½ of a 21-ounce can cherry pie filling
1 tablespoon Amaretto
⅛ teaspoon ground nutmeg
Dairy sour cream
Ground cinnamon

Place waffles on rack in oven. Toast at medium setting. Meanwhile, in a saucepan combine pie filling, Amaretto, and nutmeg. Cook over low heat for 2 to 3 minutes. Stack 2 waffles on an individual serving plate. Spoon ¼ of the cherry mixture over waffles. Dollop with sour cream; sprinkle lightly with cinnamon. Repeat for remaining servings. Makes 4 servings.

Crunchy-Top Pound Cake

1 tablespoon maple-flavored syrup
2 tablespoons butter *or* margarine, softened
½ loaf frozen pound cake, thawed and cut into 4 slices
¼ cup chopped walnuts *or* sliced almonds
2 tablespoons coconut

Stir syrup into butter or margarine till well blended. Spread butter mixture on 1 side of each cake slice. Sprinkle with nuts and coconut. Place cake slices, topping side up, on rack in oven. Toast at medium setting till topping is lightly browned. Makes 4 servings.

Brown Bread Shortcakes
Cherry-Topped Waffles
Crunchy-Top Pound Cake

BAKING

All the things you like to bake in a conventional oven you can bake in your toaster oven. Pictured here are *Leek-Artichoke Appetizer Pie, Bulgur Beef Roll, Baked Turkey Sandwich, Chicken Nut Bites,* and *Carrot Cake Loaves*—good examples of the variety of recipes you'll find in this chapter (see index for recipe pages). But there's more. Hearty main dishes, casseroles, yeast and quick breads, first-course pleasers, baked vegetables, and fancy desserts all have been sized for toaster oven cooking without sacrificing creativity or good taste.

Leek-Artichoke Appetizer Pie

Pictured on pages 14 and 15. Prepare this elegant first course in a pie plate or a rectangular baking dish—

Appetizer Pie Pastry
(see recipe, right)
1 cup chopped leeks
(2 large)
2 tablespoons butter *or* margarine
1 3-ounce package cream cheese, softened
2 eggs
¼ cup milk
⅛ teaspoon salt
Dash ground red pepper
1 6-ounce jar artichoke hearts, drained and finely chopped
1 2½-ounce jar sliced mushrooms, drained

Prepare pastry shell; set aside. In a saucepan cook chopped leeks in the butter or margarine till tender but not brown. In mixer bowl beat softened cream cheese till fluffy. Add eggs, milk, salt, and ground red pepper; beat till blended. Stir in cooked leeks, chopped artichokes, and mushrooms.

Turn artichoke mixture into prebaked pastry shell. Bake in a 350° oven for 35 to 40 minutes. Let stand 10 minutes before serving. Cut into wedges or rectangles. Serve warm. Makes 6 servings.

Appetizer Pie Pastry

¾ cup all-purpose flour
¼ teaspoon salt
¼ cup shortening *or* lard
2 to 3 tablespoons cold water

In medium mixing bowl stir together flour and salt. Cut in shortening or lard till pieces are the size of small peas. Sprinkle *1 tablespoon* cold water over part of the mixture; gently toss with a fork. Push to side of mixing bowl. Repeat till all is moistened. Form dough into a ball. On lightly floured surface flatten dough with hands.

For 7-inch pastry shell, roll dough from center to edge, forming a circle about 10 inches in diameter. Wrap pastry around rolling pin. Unroll onto a 7-inch pie plate. Ease pastry into pie plate, being careful to avoid stretching pastry. Trim crust to ½ inch beyond edge. Crimp edge.

For rectangular pastry shell, roll dough into a 10x8½-inch rectangle. Wrap pastry around rolling pin. Unroll onto an 8x6½x2-inch baking dish. Ease pastry into dish; avoid stretching pastry. Trim sides.

Do not prick pastry shell. Bake pastry in a 450° oven for 5 minutes. Makes one 7-inch round or one 8x6½x2-inch rectangular single-crust pastry.

HOW TO MAKE SHRIMP SPIRALS

To prevent sticking, place the thawed puff pastry on a pastry cloth. Roll the pastry to a 15x10-inch rectangle. Spread the shrimp and cream cheese mixture lengthwise over half the dough. Spread almost to the edges.

Fold the pastry in half over the filling to make a 15x5-inch rectangle. Press edges to seal. Cut filled pastry crosswise into 15 one-inch-wide strips.

Hold each strip at both ends and twist in opposite directions twice to form a spiral. Place spirals, several at a time, on an ungreased baking tray; press ends down. Bake in a 450° oven about 10 minutes.

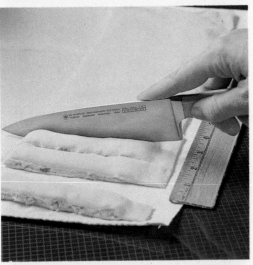

17

Shrimp Spirals

- 1 4½-ounce can shrimp, rinsed, drained, and finely chopped
- 1 4-ounce container whipped cream cheese with chives
- 2 tablespoons finely chopped pimiento
- ½ of a 17¼-ounce package frozen puff pastry, thawed

Combine shrimp, cheese, and pimiento. Roll out pastry to a 15x10-inch rectangle. Spread shrimp mixture lengthwise over half the pastry. Fold in half over mixture to a 15x5-inch rectangle. Cut into 15 one-inch-wide strips. Holding each strip at both ends, twist in opposite directions twice, forming a spiral. Place on ungreased baking tray, pressing ends down. Bake in a 450° oven about 10 minutes. Drain on paper toweling. Makes 15.

Mexican Crescents

- 4 9-inch flour tortillas
- 1 medium avocado
- 1 tablespoon chopped onion
- ⅛ teaspoon chili powder
- 2 to 3 tablespoons taco sauce
- 2 tablespoons butter, melted
  Garlic salt

Cut tortillas into 8 wedges. Seed, peel, and mash avocado; add onion and chili powder. Stir in enough taco sauce to achieve desired consistency. Spoon about 1 teaspoon mixture on each wedge. Beginning at wide end, roll toward point. Place, point down, on baking tray. Brush with butter; sprinkle with garlic salt. Bake in a 400° oven about 12 minutes. Makes 32.

TOASTING NUTS, SEEDS, AND COCONUT

Your toaster oven is the perfect appliance for toasting small quantities of nuts, seeds, and coconut. To toast nuts or seeds, spread in a single layer on the baking tray. Bake in a 350° oven for 10 to 15 minutes, stirring often. Toast coconut by spreading it in a single layer on the baking tray and baking in a 350° oven for 6 to 7 minutes, stirring twice. Use toasted pumpkin or sesame seeds for snacking, in salads, or for main-dish garnishes. Coconut and toasted nuts, especially almonds, pecans, and walnuts, make tasty, crunchy toppers for frosted cakes and cookies, sauces, puddings, and ice cream.

Pumpkin-Cashew Crunch

    1½ cups cashews
      1 cup shelled pumpkin seed
      1 tablespoon grated
        Parmesan cheese
     ½ teaspoon chili powder
     ½ teaspoon onion powder
      1 tablespoon butter, melted

Combine cashews, pumpkin seed, Parmesan cheese, chili powder, and onion powder. Drizzle with butter; toss till well coated. Spread in a single layer on ungreased baking tray. Bake in a 350° oven for 10 to 14 minutes, stirring often. Makes 2½ cups.

Chicken-Nut Bites

Pictured on pages 14 and 15

     ½ cup chicken broth
     ¼ cup butter or margarine
     ½ cup all-purpose flour
      1 tablespoon snipped parsley
     ½ teaspoon celery seed
        Dash ground red pepper
      2 eggs
     ½ cup finely chopped cooked
        chicken
      2 tablespoons chopped
        toasted almonds

Bring broth and butter to boiling. Stir in flour, parsley, celery seed, and red pepper. Cook, stirring vigorously, till mixture leaves sides of pan and forms a smooth, compact ball. Remove from heat. Cool 10 minutes. Add eggs, one at a time, beating well after each addition till mixture is shiny. Stir in chicken and nuts. Drop by rounded teaspoonfuls onto ungreased baking tray. Bake in a 400° oven for 15 to 18 minutes. Makes 30.

Pita and Pork Wedges

     ½ pound ground pork
     ¼ cup chopped onion
    1½ cups shredded Monterey
        Jack cheese (6 ounces)
      1 3-ounce can chopped
        mushrooms, drained
      2 tablespoons chopped
        pimiento
     ½ teaspoon chili powder
     ¼ teaspoon salt
     ⅛ teaspoon ground cumin
     ⅛ teaspoon garlic powder
      4 pita bread rounds
     ½ cup crushed corn chips

In skillet combine the ground pork and the chopped onion. Cook till the meat is brown and the onion is tender. Drain off fat. Stir in the shredded Monterey Jack cheese, drained chopped mushrooms, chopped pimiento, chili powder, salt, cumin, and garlic powder. Spread ¼ of the meat-cheese mixture over top surface of each pita bread round.

Place 2 of the pita bread rounds on the baking tray. Bake in a 400° oven about 5 minutes or till cheese is bubbly. Cut each pita round into 8 wedges. Sprinkle wedges with half of the crushed corn chips. Repeat with the remaining pita bread rounds. Arrange the appetizer wedges on a serving plate. Serve hot. Makes 32 appetizers.

Blue Cheese Appetizer Bits

- 1 cup all-purpose flour
- ¾ teaspoon baking powder
- ½ teaspoon caraway seed
- ¼ teaspoon onion powder
- 1 5-ounce jar blue cheese spread
- ¼ cup milk

In bowl combine flour, baking powder, caraway seed, and onion powder. Cut in cheese spread till mixture resembles coarse crumbs. Make a well in center; add milk all at once. Stir just till mixture clings together. Drop from a teaspoon onto ungreased baking tray. Bake in a 400° oven for 12 to 15 minutes. Makes about 30 appetizers.

Turkey-Ham Snack Balls

- 1 beaten egg
- 1 tablespoon chili sauce
- 1 tablespoon prepared mustard
- 1 cup soft bread crumbs
- 2 tablespoons finely chopped onion
- ⅛ teaspoon ground ginger
- ½ pound ground raw turkey
- 1 3-ounce can deviled ham
- ½ cup crushed rich round crackers

In bowl combine egg, chili sauce, and mustard. Stir in bread crumbs, onion, and ginger. Add turkey and ham; mix well. Shape into 1-inch meatballs. Roll in crushed crackers. Place half on baking tray; chill remaining meatballs. Bake in a 400° oven about 15 minutes. Repeat with remaining meatballs. Serve with additional warmed chili sauce, if desired. Makes 28 meatballs.

Sausage Pizza Appetizers

- ½ pound bulk Italian sausage
- ¼ cup chopped green pepper
- ½ of a 4-ounce container whipped cream cheese
- 2 tablespoons milk
- 1 tablespoon grated Parmesan cheese
- ⅛ teaspoon dried oregano, crushed
- 1 package (6) refrigerated biscuits
- ½ cup tomato sauce
  Sliced pimiento-stuffed olives

In skillet cook Italian sausage and green pepper till sausage is brown and green pepper is tender; drain off fat. In a small bowl combine the whipped cream cheese, milk, Parmesan cheese, and dried oregano; set aside.

On a lightly floured surface roll out each biscuit to a 4-inch circle. Place 3 of the biscuit circles on a greased baking tray. Spread about 1 tablespoon of the tomato sauce evenly over each biscuit. Sprinkle each with about ¼ cup of the meat mixture; drizzle with about 1 tablespoon of the cream cheese mixture. Bake in a 425° oven for 8 to 10 minutes or till crust is brown and cheese mixture is lightly browned. Repeat with remaining biscuits. To serve, cut each pizza into quarters and garnish with an olive slice. Makes 24 appetizers.

Oven Burgundy Stew

1 **pound beef stew meat, cut into 1-inch cubes**
4 **slices bacon, cut in pieces**
1 **large onion, thinly sliced**
2 **cloves garlic, minced**
2 **medium carrots, sliced**
2 **small stalks celery, cut up**
½ **teaspoon instant beef bouillon granules**
1 **cup burgundy *or* dry red wine**
1 **tablespoon quick-cooking tapioca**
2 **tablespoons snipped parsley**

In a small skillet brown beef stew meat, bacon, sliced onion, and minced garlic. In a 1-quart casserole combine the carrot slices, celery, instant beef bouillon granules, and the meat mixture.

Combine the burgundy or dry red wine and the tapioca; let stand for 5 minutes. Stir in the snipped parsley. Pour the wine mixture over the ingredients in the casserole.

Cover the casserole and bake in a 400° oven about 1¾ hours or till meat and vegetables are tender. Stir the stew once halfway through the baking time to keep the meat from drying out. Makes 4 servings.

Beer-Beef Bake

½ **pound beef round steak**
¼ **cup sliced green onion**
1 **clove garlic, minced**
1 **tablespoon cooking oil**
1 **tablespoon all-purpose flour**
1 **teaspoon instant beef bouillon granules**
¼ **teaspoon dried thyme, crushed**
¾ **cup beer**
 Hot cooked noodles *or* rice

Partially freeze meat; cut into thin strips. Cook meat, onion, and garlic in oil till meat is brown. Stir in flour, bouillon granules, thyme, and ⅛ teaspoon *pepper*. Add beer; cook and stir till bubbly. Turn into a 20-ounce casserole. Bake covered, in a 350° oven about 1 hour. Skim off fat. Serve over noodles or rice. Makes 2 servings.

Beef Turnovers

3 **frozen patty shells**
1 **cup chopped cooked beef**
⅓ **cup packaged instant mashed potato flakes**
⅓ **cup chopped onion**
1 **hard-cooked egg, chopped**
¼ **cup milk**
1 **teaspoon Worcestershire sauce**

Thaw patty shells in refrigerator several hours or overnight. On floured surface roll each shell to a 7-inch circle. Combine next 6 ingredients, ⅛ teaspoon *salt*, and dash *pepper*. Place about ½ cup mixture on *half* of each circle. Fold in half. Brush edges with more milk; seal. Brush tops with more milk. Place on baking tray. Bake in a 400° oven about 30 minutes. Serve with warmed catsup, if desired. Makes 3 servings.

Bulgur Beef Roll

Pictured on pages 14 and 15 —

- **¼ cup bulgur wheat**
- **¼ cup shredded carrot**
- **¼ teaspoon onion powder**
- **⅛ teaspoon dried dillweed**
- **½ pound beef round steak**
- **2 slices mozzarella cheese**
- **1 tablespoon all-purpose flour**
- **⅛ teaspoon garlic salt**
  Dash pepper
- **2 tablespoons cooking oil**
- **1 8-ounce can tomato sauce**
- **1 tablespoon dry white wine**
  Green onion curls *or* parsley sprigs

In bowl combine bulgur and ½ cup warm *water*; let stand 1 hour. Drain well, pressing out excess water. Stir in carrot, onion powder, and dillweed; set aside.

Cover meat with plastic wrap. Pound meat to ¼-inch thickness. Place cheese slices atop meat. Spread bulgur mixture over cheese slices. Roll up jelly-roll style, beginning with short side. Skewer or tie to secure roll.

Combine flour, garlic salt, and pepper; coat meat roll. In skillet brown meat on all sides in hot cooking oil. Transfer meat to 7½x3½x2-inch loaf pan. Combine tomato sauce and wine; pour half over meat. Set remaining mixture aside. Cover meat and bake in a 350° oven about 1 hour or till meat is tender. Transfer meat to serving platter. Heat remaining tomato mixture and spoon over meat. Garnish with green onion or parsley. To serve, cut into slices. Makes 2 servings.

HOW TO MAKE BULGUR BEEF ROLL

Place the piece of beef round steak on a cutting board. Cover the meat with clear plastic wrap to prevent splattering. Then, pound the meat with a meat mallet until it is ¼ inch thick. Use firm hard strokes. Move the mallet across the meat until it is of uniform thickness.

Place sliced mozzarella cheese atop the pounded meat. Spread the bulgur-carrot mixture over the cheese. Roll up the meat jelly-roll style, starting from the short side. Skewer or tie the meat roll to secure it.

German-Style Meatballs

¾ cup soft bread crumbs (1 slice)
3 tablespoons milk
2 tablespoons finely chopped onion
½ teaspoon prepared mustard
¼ teaspoon salt
  Dash pepper
½ pound ground beef
1 2-ounce can chopped mushrooms, drained
2 gingersnaps, coarsely crushed
½ teaspoon instant beef bouillon granules
½ cup water

In a small mixing bowl combine the bread crumbs, milk, the finely chopped onion, prepared mustard, salt, and pepper; add ground beef and mix well. Shape the ground beef mixture into 6 meatballs. Place in a 7x5½x2-inch baking pan. Bake, uncovered, in a 375° oven for 30 minutes. Drain.

In a small saucepan combine the chopped mushrooms, crushed gingersnaps, and instant beef bouillon granules; stir in water. Cook and stir over medium heat till mixture is thickened and bubbly. Pour over meatballs. Bake, uncovered, about 10 minutes more or till meatballs are done. Makes 2 servings.

Ham Biscuit Crescent

¾ cup packaged biscuit mix
2 tablespoons cornmeal
1 teaspoon sesame seed
¼ cup milk
1 4½-ounce can deviled ham
1 2-ounce can chopped mushrooms, drained
2 tablespoons sliced green onion
½ cup dairy sour cream
  Milk
1 tablespoon milk
2 teaspoons prepared mustard

In bowl combine biscuit mix, cornmeal, and sesame seed; add the ¼ cup milk. Stir with fork just till dough follows fork around bowl. On lightly floured surface knead dough 10 to 12 times. Roll or pat to a 9x6-inch rectangle.

Combine ham, drained mushrooms, onion, and 2 tablespoons of the sour cream; spread evenly over dough. Roll up dough jelly-roll style, beginning at long side; seal long seam. Place, seam side down, on greased baking tray. Make cuts at 1-inch intervals from side of roll to within ½ inch of opposite side. Form roll into a semicircle pulling sections apart slightly. Brush with a little additional milk. Bake in a 375° oven about 25 minutes.

Meanwhile, combine the remaining sour cream, the 1 tablespoon milk, and the mustard; mix well. Pass with meat roll. Makes 3 or 4 servings.

Note: You may substitute 1 to 2 tablespoons prepared horseradish for the mustard.

Ham Biscuit Crescent
Baked Ham and Cabbage Rolls
(see recipe, page 24)

FREEZING CREPES

Use leftover crepes as "planned-overs" for elegant entrées without all the fuss. Fresh, unfilled crepes freeze well, and they'll keep for two to four months in the freezer. Simply stack crepes, alternating each crepe with two layers of waxed paper. The paper makes for easy separating later. Then place stacked crepes in a moisture-vaporproof bag; seal. For extra protection in the freezer, place wrapped crepes in a plastic or glass container. Remove crepes as desired. Let thaw at room temperature for one hour before using.

Fruited Ham Crepes

6 Main Dish Crepes (see recipe below)
½ cup crushed pineapple, drained
1 3-ounce package cream cheese with chives
1 cup diced fully cooked ham
¼ medium green pepper, thinly sliced
1 tablespoon butter *or* margarine
1 tablespoon lemon juice

Prepare Main Dish Crepes; set aside. Combine drained pineapple and cream cheese; stir in ham. For each crepe place ham-pineapple mixture in center of unbrowned side of crepe; roll up. Place, seam side down, on baking tray. Cook sliced green pepper in butter or margarine till tender but not brown. Stir in lemon juice; spoon over crepes. Cover and bake in a 375° oven about 20 minutes. Serves 3.

Main Dish Crepes

½ cup all-purpose flour
¾ cup milk
1 egg
2 teaspoons cooking oil
⅛ teaspoon salt

Beat flour, milk, egg, cooking oil, and salt till blended. Heat a lightly greased 6-inch skillet. Remove from heat; spoon in 2 tablespoons batter. Lift and tilt skillet to spread batter. Return to heat; brown on one side. Invert onto paper toweling. Repeat with remaining batter. Makes 8 crepes.

Baked Ham and Cabbage Rolls

Pictured on page 23 —

2 cups chopped cabbage
¼ cup shredded Swiss cheese (1 ounce)
4 slices boiled ham (4 ounces)
1 tablespoon chopped onion
1 tablespoon butter *or* margarine
1 tablespoon all-purpose flour
Dash pepper
⅔ cup milk
1 teaspoon horseradish mustard
¼ cup shredded Swiss cheese (1 ounce)
1 tablespoon snipped parsley
⅓ cup soft bread crumbs
1 tablespoon butter *or* margarine, melted

Cook cabbage, covered, in a small amount of boiling salted water for 9 to 10 minutes or till tender; drain. Place about ⅓ cup cooked cabbage and 1 tablespoon cheese on each ham slice; roll up ham from short side. Place, seam side down, in a shallow baking dish.

In saucepan cook onion in 1 tablespoon butter or margarine till tender; stir in flour and pepper. Add milk and mustard; cook and stir till thickened and bubbly. Stir in ¼ cup cheese and parsley till cheese is melted. Pour over ham rolls. Top with mixture of crumbs and 1 tablespoon melted butter. Bake, uncovered, in a 375° oven about 15 minutes. Makes 2 servings.

Apple-Raisin Stuffed Chops

3 pork loin rib chops, cut 1 inch thick
2 tablespoons raisins *or* dried currants
2 tablespoons hot water
1 small apple, cored and finely chopped
1 tablespoon chopped walnuts
1 teaspoon lemon juice
½ teaspoon sugar
¼ teaspoon salt
⅛ teaspoon ground ginger
Dash ground cloves
1 slice bread, toasted and cubed (about ¾ cup)
1 to 2 tablespoons dry white wine

Cut a pocket in the fat side of each chop, cutting to the bone. Set aside. Combine raisins or currants and hot water; let stand 5 minutes. Add chopped apple, walnuts, lemon juice, sugar, salt, ginger, and cloves; mix well. Stir bread cubes into apple mixture. Lightly toss with enough wine to moisten. Spoon about ⅓ cup of the apple mixture into the pocket.

Place chops in a shallow baking pan; sprinkle with a little salt and pepper. Cover with foil; bake in a 350° oven for 1 hour. Uncover; bake 15 to 20 minutes more or till done. Garnish with additional apple slices or parsley sprigs, if desired. Makes 3 servings.

Taco Pork Chops

2 pork chops, cut ½ inch thick
½ cup finely crushed cheese-flavored tortilla chips
⅓ cup catsup
2 teaspoons butter *or* margarine
¼ teaspoon chili powder
¼ teaspoon ground cumin
Few dashes bottled hot pepper sauce
Dash garlic powder

Trim excess fat from chops. Dip chops in crushed chips, coating both sides evenly. Spray baking tray with non-stick vegetable spray coating. Place chops on tray. Bake in a 350° oven about 45 minutes or till done. Meanwhile, in saucepan stir together remaining ingredients. Cook and stir till heated through and butter is melted. Serve over chops. Makes 2 servings.

Meal in a Spud

1 medium baking potato
Horseradish mustard
2 ounces sliced Canadian-style bacon, halved crosswise
½ small tomato, sliced
1 ounce sliced cheese, quartered

Scrub potato but do not peel. Cut crosswise into 5 slices. Place on a square of foil; wrap securely. Bake in a 425° oven for 40 to 50 minutes. Unwrap; separate slices slightly. Spread cut surfaces of potato liberally with horseradish mustard. Place a bacon and tomato slice between each potato slice. Wrap with foil. Return to 400° oven; bake 10 minutes. Open foil; insert cheese between bacon and tomato. Return to oven; bake till cheese melts. Makes 1 serving.

Easy Pork Tetrazzini

There's no need to precook the spaghetti for this tasty casserole—

- ½ **pound ground pork**
- 1 **3-ounce package cream cheese, softened**
- ⅓ **cup milk**
- ¼ **cup chopped green onion**
- ¼ **cup grated Parmesan cheese**
- ⅛ **teaspoon salt**
  Dash ground nutmeg
  Dash pepper
- ⅔ **cup boiling water**
- 2 **ounces uncooked spaghetti broken into 1- to 2-inch lengths**
  Thinly sliced green onion (optional)

In small skillet cook the ground pork till brown; drain well. In a small bowl combine the softened cream cheese and milk till smooth. Stir in chopped green onion, *half* of the grated Parmesan cheese, the salt, nutmeg, and pepper. Gradually stir in the boiling water. Stir in pork and uncooked spaghetti. Turn into two 10- or 12-ounce casseroles.

Cover and bake in a 350° oven about 1 hour or till meat and spaghetti are done, stirring twice. Uncover casseroles and sprinkle with remaining grated Parmesan cheese. If desired, garnish with green onion slices. Makes 2 servings.

Frankfurter Salad Sandwiches

You can substitute ⅔ cup chopped precooked sausage links or bologna for the frankfurters—

- 2 **frankfurters, coarsely chopped**
- 1 **hard-cooked egg, chopped**
- ½ **cup shredded cheddar cheese (2 ounces)**
- ¼ **cup chopped celery**
- 2 **tablespoons thinly sliced green onion**
- 2 **tablespoons mayonnaise** *or* **salad dressing**
- 1 **teaspoon dried parsley flakes**
- 1 **teaspoon prepared mustard**
- 2 **French-style rolls**

In a small bowl combine the chopped frankfurters, the chopped egg, *¼ cup* of the shredded cheese, the chopped celery, the thinly sliced green onion, mayonnaise or salad dressing, dried parsley flakes, and prepared mustard.

Cut a thin slice off the top of each loaf of French bread. Hollow out the centers of the loaves, leaving a shell about ½ inch thick. Fill shells with frankfurter mixture.

Wrap each sandwich in foil and bake in a 350° oven about 25 minutes or till heated through. Open foil. Sprinkle sandwiches with the remaining shredded cheddar cheese. Continue baking 2 to 3 minutes more or till cheese melts. Makes 2 servings.

Macaroni and Sausage Casserole

- ⅓ cup elbow macaroni
- 2 tablespoons chopped onion
- 1 tablespoon butter *or* margarine
- 4 teaspoons all-purpose flour
- 1 cup milk
- ½ cup shredded cheddar *or* American cheese
- ½ cup frozen peas
- 2 fully cooked smoked sausage links, sliced (½ cup)
- 2 tablespoons chopped pimiento
- ¼ cup crushed rich round crackers

Cook macaroni according to package directions. Drain; set aside. In saucepan cook the chopped onion in the butter or margarine till tender but not brown. Stir in flour. Add milk; cook and stir till thickened and bubbly. Stir in shredded cheese till melted. Stir in cooked macaroni, peas, sliced sausage, and chopped pimiento.

Turn the mixture into two 10-ounce casseroles. Sprinkle crushed crackers atop casseroles. Bake, uncovered, in a 350° oven for 20 to 25 minutes. Makes 2 servings.

Frank Manicotti Olé

- 5 manicotti shells
- 5 frankfurters
- 1 8¼-ounce can refried beans
- 1 cup chili salsa
- ½ cup shredded Monterey Jack cheese (2 ounces)

Cook manicotti shells according to package directions; drain. Place 1 frank inside each cooked manicotti shell. Spread refried beans in bottom of an 8x6½x2-inch baking dish. Arrange the filled shells atop beans; pour salsa over. Cover; bake in a 350° oven for 35 minutes. Uncover; sprinkle with cheese. Bake, uncovered, about 5 minutes more or till cheese is melted. Makes 3 servings.

Sausage Spoon Bread

- ¼ cup all-purpose flour
- ¼ cup yellow cornmeal
- 1 teaspoon sugar
- ½ teaspoon baking powder
- 1 beaten egg
- 1 8-ounce can cream-style corn
- ¼ pound bulk pork sausage, cooked and drained
- ¼ cup shredded Swiss cheese

Combine flour, cornmeal, sugar, and baking powder. Stir in egg, corn, and cooked sausage. Turn mixture into a 15- or 16-ounce baking dish. Bake, uncovered, in a 350° oven about 40 minutes or till knife inserted between center and edge comes out clean. Sprinkle with shredded cheese. Bake 2 to 3 minutes more or till cheese is melted. Serves 2.

Spicy Sausage and Cheese Casserole

Serve this strata-like, make-ahead dish for brunch or supper—

- ¼ pound bulk Italian sausage
- 1 cup crushed tortilla chips
- 2 beaten eggs
- ¾ cup milk
- ¼ teaspoon chili powder
- ½ cup shredded cheddar cheese (2 ounces)

In small skillet cook Italian sausage till brown; drain off fat. Set sausage aside. Sprinkle *half* of the crushed tortilla chips evenly in the bottoms of 2 greased 1½-cup individual casseroles. Top with the cooked sausage; sprinkle with the remaining tortilla chips.

Combine eggs, milk, and chili powder. Pour the egg-milk mixture over the layers in the casseroles. Sprinkle with the shredded cheddar cheese. Cover casseroles and chill in the refrigerator several hours or overnight.

Bake, uncovered, in a 350° oven about 40 minutes or till a knife inserted in the center comes clean. Let casseroles stand for 5 minutes before serving. Makes 2 servings.

Breakfast Burritos

- ¼ pound bulk pork sausage
- 2 tablespoons finely chopped onion
- 2 tablespoons finely chopped green pepper
- 2 eggs
- 2 tablespoons milk
- ⅛ teaspoon salt
  Dash pepper
- 1 tablespoon butter *or* margarine
- 4 6- or 7-inch flour tortillas
- 1 small tomato, peeled, seeded, and chopped
- ½ cup shredded cheddar cheese (2 ounces)

In skillet cook pork sausage, onion, and green pepper till meat is brown and onion and green pepper are tender. Drain off fat; set aside. In a bowl beat together eggs, milk, salt, and pepper. In an 8- or 10-inch skillet melt butter or margarine over medium heat; pour in egg mixture. Cook, without stirring, till mixture begins to set on the bottom and around edges. Using a large spoon or spatula, lift and fold partially cooked eggs so uncooked portion flows underneath. Continue cooking over medium heat till eggs are almost cooked throughout. Remove from heat.

Spoon ¼ of the meat mixture onto each tortilla near one edge. Top with cooked eggs and chopped tomato. Roll tortilla around filling. If necessary, secure with a wooden pick. Arrange on baking tray. Sprinkle with cheese. Bake in 350° oven about 15 minutes or till heated through. Makes 2 servings

Minty Lamb Casserole

- 1 pound ground lamb
- ½ cup chopped onion
- 1 clove garlic, minced
- 3 tablespoons butter *or* margarine
- 3 tablespoons all-purpose flour
- ½ teaspoon salt
- ¼ teaspoon dried mint, crushed, *or* ¾ teaspoon snipped fresh mint
- ¼ teaspoon dried oregano, crushed
- 1½ cups milk
- 3 beaten eggs
- 1 10-ounce package frozen chopped spinach, thawed and drained
- 1 cup cooked rice
- ½ cup crumbled feta cheese

In skillet cook lamb, onion, and garlic till meat is brown and onion is tender; drain off fat. In a small saucepan melt butter or margarine. Stir in flour, salt, mint, and oregano. Add milk all at once; cook and stir till thickened and bubbly. Cook and stir 1 minute more. Gradually stir the thickened milk mixture into beaten eggs.

Combine the lamb mixture, spinach, cooked rice, and feta cheese. Stir in hot milk-egg mixture. Turn mixture into an 8x6½x2-inch baking dish. Bake in a 325° oven for 45 to 50 minutes. Makes 6 servings.

Cheese-Topped Lamb Chops

- 3 lamb leg sirloin chops cut 1 inch thick (1 pound total)
- 1 tablespoon cooking oil
- 2 tablespoons butter *or* margarine
- 2 tablespoons all-purpose flour
- ⅓ cup milk
- 1 beaten egg
- ¼ cup grated Parmesan cheese
- 1 teaspoon grated onion
- ⅛ teaspoon pepper
  Paprika

In skillet slowly brown lamb chops on both sides in hot oil about 10 minutes. Drain well; transfer chops to baking tray. In a small saucepan melt the butter or margarine; stir in the all-purpose flour. Add milk; cook and stir till mixture is thickened and bubbly. Stir *half* of the thickened mixture into the beaten egg; return to saucepan. Cook for 1 minute more, stirring mixture constantly.

Stir in grated Parmesan cheese, onion, and pepper. Spoon mixture atop each chop. Sprinkle with paprika. Bake, uncovered, in a 350° oven about 30 minutes or till meat is done and topping is lightly browned. Remove to serving plates. Makes 3 servings.

Chicken Livers and Wild Rice Bake

This casserole serves six and is fancy enough for a dinner party—

- 1 6-ounce package long grain and wild rice mix
- ½ cup chopped onion
- 2 tablespoons butter *or* margarine
- 1 pound chicken livers, halved
- 1 4-ounce container whipped cream cheese
- ¼ cup milk
- ¼ teaspoon dried basil, crushed
- 1 10-ounce package frozen cut asparagus, thawed
- ¾ cup soft bread crumbs (1 slice)
- 1 tablespoon butter *or* margarine, melted

Prepare the rice mix according to package directions; set aside. In a skillet cook chopped onion in 2 tablespoons butter or margarine till tender but not brown. Stir in halved chicken livers; cook till livers are just barely pink. Stir in whipped cream cheese, milk, and basil. Stir in thawed asparagus and cooked rice. Turn mixture into an 8x6½x2-inch baking dish.

Combine bread crumbs and 1 tablespoon melted butter or margarine; sprinkle over rice mixture. Bake, uncovered, in a 350° oven for 30 to 35 minutes or till the casserole is heated through. Makes 6 servings.

Curried Apple-Chicken Scallop

- 2 medium apples, cored and chopped
- ½ cup finely chopped onion
- ½ cup finely chopped celery
- 1 teaspoon curry powder
- 2 tablespoons cooking oil
- 3 tablespoons all-purpose flour
- ½ teaspoon salt
- ⅛ teaspoon pepper
- 1½ cups milk
- 1 16-ounce can sliced potatoes, drained
- 2 cups chopped cooked chicken
- ¼ cup crushed rich round crackers
- ¼ cup chopped peanuts

In skillet cook apple, onion, celery, and curry powder, covered, in hot oil over medium heat about 5 minutes or till tender. Stir in flour, salt, and pepper. Add milk. Cook and stir till thickened and bubbly. Remove from heat. In an 8x6½x2-inch baking dish, layer half the potatoes and half the chicken. Pour half the apple mixture atop. Repeat layers. Bake, covered, in a 350° oven for 25 to 30 minutes or till heated through. Uncover; sprinkle with crushed crackers and peanuts. Bake about 5 minutes more. Makes 4 servings.

Chicken a l'Orange

- 2 chicken thighs
- 1 tablespoon dry white wine
- 2 teaspoons brown sugar
- 2 teaspoons sliced green onion
- 1 teaspoon finely shredded orange peel
- ⅛ teaspoon dried rosemary, crushed

Place chicken thighs on a 12x12-inch piece of foil. Turn up edges of foil. Combine wine, brown sugar, onion, orange peel, and rosemary; spoon over chicken thighs. Bring up sides of foil, folding twice to seal; seal ends. Bake in a 350° oven about 45 minutes or till chicken is tender. Remove from foil packet to serve. Serves 1.

Barbecue Chicken

- 4 chicken drumsticks
- 2 tablespoons catsup
- 2 tablespoons water
- 1 teaspoon vinegar
- 1 teaspoon Worcestershire sauce
- ½ cup shredded Monterey Jack cheese (2 ounces)
- ¼ cup finely crushed corn chips

Place chicken drumsticks in shallow baking pan. Bake, uncovered, in a 400° oven for 15 minutes. Combine catsup, water, vinegar, and Worcestershire sauce. Spoon over chicken. Turn chicken pieces to coat evenly with sauce. Bake 20 to 25 minutes longer or till chicken is tender. Sprinkle with cheese and corn chips; return to oven. Bake for 3 to 5 minutes more. Serves 2.

Chutney-Stuffed Chicken

- 1 whole medium chicken breast, skinned, halved lengthwise, and boned
- ¼ cup cooked rice
- 3 tablespoons chutney
- 2 tablespoons chopped peanuts
- ⅛ teaspoon onion powder
- 1 tablespoon butter *or* margarine
- 2 tablespoons orange juice
- 1 tablespoon soy sauce
- 1 teaspoon snipped parsley

Place halved chicken breasts between 2 pieces of clear plastic wrap. Pound out from center with meat mallet to form each into a ½x5½-inch square. Remove plastic wrap.

For stuffing, combine cooked rice, chutney, chopped peanuts, and onion powder. Spoon about ¼ cup of the stuffing onto each piece of chicken. Fold in the sides; roll up jelly-roll style. Place chicken rolls, seam side down, in a shallow baking pan.

For basting sauce, melt butter or margarine; stir in orange juice, soy sauce, and snipped parsley. Bake chicken rolls in a 400° oven about 20 minutes or till tender, basting with sauce once or twice. Place chicken rolls on serving platter. Brush with any remaining sauce before serving. Makes 2 servings.

Cheesy Chicken Loaf

1 beaten egg
¾ cup soft bread crumbs (1 slice)
¼ cup shredded carrot
1 tablespoon thinly sliced green onion
⅛ teaspoon pepper
1 5-ounce can chunk-style chicken, drained and chopped
½ cup shredded cheddar cheese (2 ounces)
1 tablespoon butter *or* margarine
¼ cup slivered almonds
2 tablespoons all-purpose flour
½ teaspoon instant chicken bouillon granules
½ cup milk

In mixing bowl combine beaten egg, soft bread crumbs, shredded carrot, green onion, and pepper. Add chopped chicken and shredded cheddar cheese; mix well. Divide chicken mixture between 2 well-greased 4½x2½x1½-inch loaf pans. Bake in a 350° oven about 25 minutes or till done.

Meanwhile, in small saucepan melt butter or margarine; add almonds. Cook and stir till nuts are toasted. Blend in flour and instant chicken bouillon granules. Add milk all at once. Cook and stir till thickened and bubbly; cook and stir 1 minute more. Invert chicken loaves onto serving plates. Spoon sauce over. Makes 2 servings.

Turkey Stew and Cornmeal Dumplings

2 tablespoons chopped onion
2 tablespoons butter *or* margarine
2 tablespoons all-purpose flour
1 teaspoon instant chicken bouillon granules
¼ teaspoon ground coriander
⅛ teaspoon chili powder
Dash pepper
1 cup milk
1 8¾-ounce can whole kernel corn, drained
1 cup chopped cooked turkey *or* chicken
1 medium tomato, peeled, seeded, and chopped
½ cup shredded cheddar cheese (2 ounces)
2 tablespoons chopped pitted ripe olives
⅔ cup all-purpose flour
⅓ cup yellow cornmeal
1 teaspoon baking powder
½ teaspoon salt
½ cup milk
2 tablespoons cooking oil

Cook onion in butter or margarine till tender but not brown. Blend in 2 tablespoons flour, the chicken bouillon granules, coriander, chili powder, and pepper. Add 1 cup milk. Cook and stir till thickened and bubbly. Stir in corn, turkey, tomato, cheese, and olives; heat till bubbly. Keep warm.

Stir together ⅔ cup flour, cornmeal, baking powder, and salt. Combine ½ cup milk and oil. Add to dry ingredients all at once; stir till moistened. Turn turkey mixture into an 8x6½x2-inch baking dish. Drop the dough from a tablespoon to make 4 mounds atop *hot* turkey mixture. Bake in a 400° oven about 15 minutes or till topping is lightly browned. Makes 4 servings.

Spicy-Hot Turkey Enchiladas

1 5-ounce can chunk-style turkey, drained
½ cup dairy sour cream
1 tablespoon sliced green onion
1 teaspoon jalapeño pepper relish
1 tablespoon cooking oil
4 6-inch flour tortillas
¼ cup tomato sauce
Dash ground red pepper
½ cup shredded Monterey Jack cheese (2 ounces)

Combine turkey, dairy sour cream, sliced green onion, and jalapeño pepper relish. In small skillet heat the cooking oil. Dip tortillas, one at a time, into the hot oil about 10 seconds or just till tortillas are limp. Drain on paper toweling.

Spoon turkey mixture onto tortillas; roll up. Place tortilla rolls, seam side down, in a shallow baking pan. Bake in a 350° oven 10 to 12 minutes or till heated through.

Combine tomato sauce and red pepper; pour atop tortilla rolls. Sprinkle with shredded Monterey Jack cheese. Return to oven. Bake about 2 minutes or till cheese melts. Makes 2 servings.

Baked Turkey Sandwich

Pictured on pages 14 and 15—

1 tablespoon butter or margarine
1 tablespoon all-purpose flour
Dash pepper
½ cup milk
½ cup shredded Swiss cheese (2 ounces)
1 tablespoon dry white wine
1 2½-ounce package very thinly sliced turkey
2 slices frozen French toast, toasted
4 thin slices tomato
4 thin slices green pepper
Grated Parmesan cheese

In small saucepan melt butter or margarine. Stir in flour and pepper. Add milk all at once. Cook and stir over medium heat till thickened and bubbly. Cook and stir 1 minute more. Over low heat stir in the Swiss cheese and wine, stirring to melt cheese. Remove from heat.

For one sandwich place half of the sliced turkey atop 1 piece French toast. Layer with half the tomato slices; top with half the green pepper slices. Repeat for the remaining sandwich. Place both sandwiches on baking tray. Pour cheese mixture over both sandwiches. Sprinkle sandwiches with Parmesan cheese. Bake in a 350° oven for 15 minutes or till heated through. Makes 2 servings.

Potato-Fish Bake

2 fresh or frozen fish fillets
¼ cup plain yogurt
4 teaspoons all-purpose flour
¼ cup milk
¼ teaspoon dried dillweed
⅛ teaspoon salt
Dash pepper
1 cup frozen hash brown potatoes with onions and peppers
¼ cup shredded Swiss cheese (1 ounce)
3 tablespoons crushed rich round crackers (5 crackers)

Thaw fish fillets, if frozen; cut fillets into cubes. In small bowl stir together the plain yogurt and all-purpose flour; gradually stir in milk, dillweed, salt, and pepper. Fold in fish cubes and hash brown potatoes. Turn fish-potato mixture into 2 individual casseroles.

Bake, covered, in a 400° oven about 40 minutes or till fish and potatoes are done. Sprinkle with shredded Swiss cheese and crushed crackers. Return to oven; bake for 3 to 5 minutes longer or till cheese is melted. Makes 2 servings.

Crispy Shrimp and Vegetables

½ pound large fresh *or* frozen shrimp in shells (10)
⅔ cup crushed crisp rice cereal
⅓ cup finely chopped cashews
⅛ teaspoon five-spice powder *or* ground ginger
4 to 6 fresh, medium whole mushrooms
1 small zucchini, cut into ½-inch slices
½ cup frozen small whole onions, thawed
3 tablespoons butter *or* margarine, melted

Thaw shrimp, if frozen. Shell and devein shrimp; set aside. Combine crushed cereal, chopped cashews, and five-spice powder or ginger. Dip shrimp and vegetables into melted butter or margarine, allowing excess to run off. Roll in the cereal mixture, pressing if necessary so coating will adhere.

Place shrimp and vegetables in a single layer on baking tray. Bake in a 450° oven for 10 to 15 minutes or till shrimp and vegetables are done and coating is crispy. Makes 2 servings.

Scallops and Crepes

6 Main Dish Crepes (see recipe, page 24)
½ pound fresh *or* frozen scallops
¾ cup whipping cream
1 tablespoon all-purpose flour
Dash salt
Dash pepper
1 2½-ounce jar sliced mushrooms, drained
2 tablespoons dry white wine *or* sherry
1 tablespoon snipped chives
2 slices bacon, crisp-cooked, drained, and crumbled
Snipped chives

Prepare crepes; set aside. Thaw scallops, if frozen. In saucepan cover scallops with cold water. Bring to boiling; reduce heat and simmer 1 minute. Drain and halve scallops.

In small saucepan gradually add whipping cream to flour, stirring till smooth. Stir in salt and pepper. Cook and stir over low heat till thickened and bubbly. Stir in mushrooms, wine, 1 tablespoon chives, and crumbled bacon. Reserve half of the mixture. Stir scallops into the remaining half of the mixture.

Spoon about ¼ cup of the scallop mixture down the center of unbrowned side of crepe; roll up. Place, seam side down, in shallow baking dish. Repeat with remaining crepes. Spoon the reserved wine mixture over crepes. Bake in a 375° oven for 15 to 18 minutes. Sprinkle with additional chives. Makes 3 servings.

Crab in Coquilles

- 2 tablespoons chopped celery
- 2 tablespoons chopped onion
- 1 tablespoon butter *or* margarine
- 1 tablespoon all-purpose flour
- ¼ teaspoon dried tarragon, crushed
  Dash pepper
- ⅓ cup milk
- 1 6-ounce can crab meat, drained, flaked, and cartilage removed
- 1 small tomato, peeled, seeded, and chopped (½ cup)
- ⅓ cup soft bread crumbs
- 1 tablespoon dry sherry
- 2 teaspoons snipped parsley
- 1 teaspoon butter *or* margarine, melted

In small saucepan cook celery and onion in the 1 tablespoon butter till tender but not brown. Stir in flour, tarragon, and pepper. Add milk. Cook and stir till thickened and bubbly. Stir in crab meat, tomato, *half* of the bread crumbs, sherry, and parsley.

Spoon crab mixture into 2 buttered coquilles (individual baking shells) or 6-ounce custard cups. Toss the remaining bread crumbs with the 1 teaspoon melted butter; sprinkle over crab mixture. Bake, uncovered, in a 400° oven for 15 to 20 minutes or till browned. Makes 2 servings.

Salmon Roll-Ups

- 1 7¾-ounce can salmon, drained, flaked, and skin and bones removed
- 2 tablespoons finely chopped green pepper
- 1 tablespoon finely chopped onion
- 2 teaspoons lemon juice
- 1 cup packaged biscuit mix
- ¼ cup milk
  Sour cream dip with French onion

Combine salmon, green pepper, onion, lemon juice, and dash *pepper*. For dough, combine biscuit mix and milk. On lightly floured surface roll dough to 12x8-inch rectangle. Cut into four 6x4-inch rectangles. Place about ¼ cup salmon mixture on each. Roll up from narrow end; seal edge. Place seam side down on greased baking tray. Bake in a 450° oven for 10 to 12 minutes. Serve with dip. Makes 2 servings.

Tuna Bagelwich

- 1 3¼-ounce can tuna
- 1 small apple, chopped
- ½ of an 8-ounce can crushed pineapple, drained
- ½ of a 4-ounce container whipped cream cheese
- 1 tablespoon chopped pecans
- 2 teaspoons mayonnaise
  Dash ground cinnamon
- 2 bagels, halved and toasted
- 4 slices Swiss cheese

Drain and flake tuna. Combine with apple, pineapple, cream cheese, pecans, mayonnaise, and cinnamon. On cut side of each bagel half, place a cheese slice. Top with tuna mixture. Bake in a 350° oven 15 to 20 minutes or till hot. Makes 2 servings.

Tuna-Topped Tater

- 1 medium baking potato
- 1 teaspoon butter *or* margarine
- ⅓ cup plain yogurt
- 1 tablespoon all-purpose flour
- ⅛ teaspoon dried oregano, crushed
- 2 tablespoons milk
- ½ cup shredded *process* Swiss cheese (2 ounces)
- 2 tablespoons finely chopped green pepper
- 1 3¼-ounce can tuna, drained and flaked
- 2 tablespoons crushed potato chips (optional)

Scrub potato with a brush. Prick potato with a fork. Bake in a 425° oven for 40 to 50 minutes. Cut potato in half lengthwise. Scoop out the insides from both halves. Mash slightly. Stir in butter; mix well. Pile potato mixture back into potato shells.

In small saucepan combine yogurt, flour, and oregano; stir in milk. Cook and stir over medium heat till thickened and bubbly. Cook and stir 1 minute more. Remove from heat. Add cheese and green pepper; stir till well blended and cheese melts. Fold in tuna.

Place potato halves in 2 au gratin dishes. Pour half of the tuna mixture over each potato half. Bake in a 425° oven for 20 to 25 minutes or till heated through and topping is lightly browned. If desired, top each potato half with 1 tablespoon crushed potato chips. Return to oven. Bake about 5 minutes more or till chips are crispy. Makes 2 servings.

36

BAKING

MAIN
DISHES

HOW TO PREPARE INDIVIDUAL QUICHES IN CREPES

Grease two 10-ounce au gratin dishes or shallow casseroles with shortening. Place two of the Main-Dish Crepes in each of the greased dishes. Overlap crepes to fit dish and ruffle top edges carefully.

Divide the chopped cooked meat between the two crepe-lined dishes. Top each with half the Italian green beans and half the shredded cheese. Pour half the egg-milk mixture over each.

Bake the quiches, uncovered, in a 350° oven for 25 to 30 minutes or till done. Test for doneness by inserting a knife near the center of each quiche. Make a short cut, about ½ inch deep; if any of the creamy egg mixture remains on the knife as it is withdrawn, bake the quiches a few minutes longer.

Individual Quiches in Crepes

- 4 Main Dish Crepes (see recipe, page 24)
- 1 beaten egg
- ⅓ cup milk
- 2 tablespoons mayonnaise *or* salad dressing
- 2 teaspoons all-purpose flour
- ⅛ teaspoon salt
  Dash ground nutmeg
- ⅓ cup chopped cooked chicken, beef, pork, *or* ham
- ½ of a 9-ounce package frozen Italian green beans, cooked and drained, *or* one 8-ounce can cut Italian green eans, drained
- ½ cup shredded Monterey Jack, mozzarella, or Swiss cheese (2 ounces)
  Cherry tomatoes, quartered (optional)
  Grated Parmesan cheese (optional)

Prepare crepes; set aside.

For filling combine beaten egg, milk, mayonnaise or salad dressing, flour, salt, and nutmeg. Place 2 of the crepes in each of 2 greased 10-ounce au gratin dishes or shallow casseroles, ruffling the top edges carefully. Divide meat between the 2 dishes. Top each with half of the green beans and half of the cheese. Divide egg mixture between casseroles, pouring over meat, green beans and cheese.

Bake, uncovered, in a 350° oven for 25 to 30 minutes or till done. Remove from oven. If desired, top each casserole with cherry tomato quarters and sprinkle with Parmesan cheese. Makes 2 servings.

Curried Ham and Egg Bake

The rye croutons you make yourself (see tip, right) can be substituted for Plain Croutons made from other types of bread —

- 4 slices boiled ham (about 3 ounces)
- 2 cups plain rye bread croutons (3 slices bread)
- 1 7½-ounce can semi-condensed mushroom soup
- ½ cup dairy sour cream
- 1 teaspoon curry powder
- 4 eggs
- ½ cup shredded process Swiss cheese (2 ounces)
  Paprika

In an 8x6½x2-inch baking dish, place the boiled ham slices in a single layer, overlapping edges slightly. Sprinkle the croutons evenly over the ham slices. Stir together the mushroom soup, sour cream, and curry powder. Pour the mushroom soup mixture over the croutons. Bake, uncovered, in a 350° oven for 20 minutes.

Remove from oven. Make 4 depressions in the crouton layer with the back of a spoon. Break eggs, one at a time, into a small dish. Carefully slide each egg into one of the depressions. Return to oven; bake 12 to 15 minutes more. Sprinkle with the shredded process Swiss cheese and paprika. Bake 2 to 3 minutes more or till cheese melts. Makes 4 servings.

MAKING CROUTONS

Transform a lone slice of bread, a spare bun, or a roll into fresh, crisp croutons for salads, snacks, or casseroles. For Plain Croutons, use sliced bread or cut buns or unsliced bread into ½-inch-thick slices. Then brush cut sides of bread lightly with cooking oil or melted butter or margarine and cut into ½-inch cubes. Place buttered cubes on foil or parchment-lined baking tray for easier cleanup. Bake the cubes in a 300° oven for 20 to 25 minutes or till cubes are dry. For Cheesy Croutons, sprinkle bread slices with grated Parmesan cheese before cutting into cubes and baking. For Herb Croutons, toss warm croutons with a light sprinkling of your favorite dried herbs. For Sesame Croutons, toss baked cubes with some toasted sesame seeds (see tip, page 18).

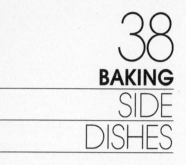

Fruited Coffee Cake

- 1 cup all-purpose flour
- ½ cup sugar
- 1 teaspoon baking powder
- ¼ teaspoon salt
- ⅓ cup butter *or* margarine
- 1 beaten egg
- ⅓ cup milk
- ½ teaspoon vanilla
- ¼ cup pineapple *or* cherry preserves
- ¼ cup packed brown sugar
- ¼ cup all-purpose flour
- 2 tablespoons butter *or* margarine
- ¼ cup sliced almonds

In mixing bowl stir together the 1 cup flour, the sugar, baking powder, and salt. Cut in the ⅓ cup butter or margarine till mixture resembles fine crumbs. Combine egg, milk, and vanilla. Add to flour mixture, stirring till blended. Spread the batter in a greased 8x6½x2-inch baking dish; dollop preserves atop by half-teaspoonfuls.

In small bowl combine the brown sugar and the ¼ cup flour; cut in the 2 tablespoons butter or margarine. Sprinkle the brown sugar mixture over batter; sprinkle with almonds. Bake in a 350° oven about 40 minutes or till the cake tests done. (If necessary cover with foil the last 10 minutes to prevent overbrowning.) Serve warm. Makes 1 coffee cake.

Apple-Nut Biscuits

- ⅓ cup sugar
- ⅓ cup chopped walnuts
- ½ teaspoon ground cinnamon
- 1⅔ cups packaged biscuit mix
- ⅓ cup chopped, peeled apple
- ⅓ cup milk
- 2 tablespoons butter, melted

Combine sugar, nuts, and cinnamon; set aside. In bowl combine biscuit mix and apple. Make a well in center of apple mixture. Add milk all at once, stirring just till moistened. Divide into 18 portions; shape into balls. Roll in melted butter, then in sugar mixture. Arrange in a greased 8x6½x2-inch baking dish or 2 greased 5x5x2-inch baking dishes. Bake in a 400° oven about 25 minutes. Remove; serve warm. Makes 18 biscuits.

Coconut-Molasses Muffins

- 1 cup all-purpose flour
- 2 tablespoons sugar
- 1 teaspoon baking powder
- ¼ teaspoon ground ginger
- ¼ cup shortening
- 1 slightly beaten egg
- ¼ cup milk
- ¼ cup light molasses
- ½ cup flaked coconut

Combine flour, sugar, baking powder, ginger, and ¼ teaspoon *salt*. Cut in shortening till mixture resembles coarse crumbs. Combine egg, milk, and molasses. Add to dry ingredients; stir just till moistened. Fold in coconut. Line muffin pan with paper bake cups; fill ⅔ full. Bake in a 350° oven for 20 to 25 minutes. Makes 6 muffins.

Cornmeal Rounds

¼ cup all-purpose flour
¼ cup yellow cornmeal
1 tablespoon sugar
½ teaspoon baking powder
Few dashes ground red pepper
1 beaten egg
3 tablespoons milk
1 tablespoon cooking oil
¼ cup shredded cheddar cheese

Combine flour, cornmeal, sugar, baking powder, red pepper, and ¼ teaspoon *salt*. Combine egg, milk, and oil; add to dry ingredients. Stir just till smooth. Stir in cheese just till combined. Turn into 2 greased 10-ounce custard cups. Bake in 425° oven about 20 minutes. Makes 2.

Poppy-Seed Muffins

2 tablespoons sugar
2 tablespoons butter
¼ teaspoon finely shredded orange peel
1 egg
¾ cup all-purpose flour
¾ teaspoon baking powder
⅛ teaspoon ground nutmeg
⅓ cup milk
¼ cup chopped pecans
2 tablespoons poppy seed

Beat sugar, butter, and orange peel with electric mixer. Add egg; beat well. Mix flour, baking powder, nutmeg, and ¼ teaspoon *salt*. Add to beaten mixture alternately with milk; beat well. Stir in nuts and poppy seed. Line muffin pan with paper bake cups; fill ⅔ full. Bake in 350° oven about 20 minutes. Makes 6.

Italian-Seasoned Drop Biscuits

¼ cup finely chopped onion
¾ teaspoon Italian seasoning
1 tablespoon butter *or* margarine
1½ cups all-purpose flour
2 teaspoons baking powder
½ teaspoon salt
¼ cup shortening
1 beaten egg
⅓ cup milk
1 tablespoon butter *or* margarine, melted
4 teaspoons grated Romano *or* Parmesan cheese

In small saucepan or skillet cook onion and Italian seasoning in 1 tablespoon butter or margarine till onion is tender but not brown. In mixing bowl thoroughly stir together the flour, baking powder, and salt. Cut in shortening till mixture resembles coarse crumbs. Combine egg, milk, and onion mixture, and add to flour mixture all at once. Stir till dough clings together. Drop dough in 8 mounds onto greased baking tray. Drizzle 1 tablespoon melted butter or margarine over the mounds of dough. Sprinkle with grated Romano or Parmesan cheese. Bake in a 450° oven for 12 to 15 minutes. Serve warm. Makes 8 biscuits.

Zucchini-Nut Loaf

1 beaten egg
½ cup shredded zucchini
⅓ cup sugar
¼ cup packed brown sugar
3 tablespoons cooking oil
2 tablespoons water
1 cup all-purpose flour
½ teaspoon baking soda
¼ teaspoon salt
¼ teaspoon ground nutmeg
¼ teaspoon ground cinnamon
⅛ teaspoon ground ginger
½ cup raisins
¼ cup chopped pecans *or* walnuts

In a medium mixing bowl combine egg, shredded zucchini, sugar, brown sugar, cooking oil and water; beat the zucchini mixture till well blended.

In small mixing bowl thoroughly stir together the all-purpose flour, baking soda, salt, ground nutmeg, cinnamon, and ginger; add to the zucchini mixture and mix well. Stir in raisins and chopped pecans or walnuts.

Turn batter into a well-greased 7½x3½x2-inch loaf pan. Bake in a 350° oven about 40 minutes or till bread is done. Cool 10 minutes in pan. Remove zucchini loaf from pan; cool on wire rack. Wrap and store loaf overnight, if desired. Makes 1 loaf.

Fennel Braid

1½ cups all-purpose flour
1 package active dry yeast
1 teaspoon fennel seed, crushed
¼ cup milk
2 tablespoons sugar
2 tablespoons butter
1 egg
½ teaspoon finely shredded lemon peel
1 tablespoon lemon juice
½ cup sifted powdered sugar
¼ teaspoon vanilla

In small mixer bowl mix ½ cup of the flour, the yeast, and fennel seed. Heat milk, sugar, butter, and ¼ teaspoon *salt* just till warm (115° to 120°); stir constantly. Add to flour mixture; add egg, lemon peel, and juice. Beat at low speed of electric mixer for ½ minute, scraping bowl constantly. Beat 3 minutes at high speed. Stir in as much remaining flour as you can mix in with a spoon. Turn out onto lightly floured surface. Knead in enough remaining flour to make a moderately soft dough that is smooth and elastic (3 to 5 minutes total). Shape into a ball. Place in lightly greased bowl; turn once. Cover; let rise in warm place till double (about 45 minutes). Punch down; divide in thirds. Cover; let rest 10 minutes. Roll each portion into a 12-inch-long rope. Line up the 3 ropes, 1 inch apart, on the greased baking tray. Braid ropes loosely. Pinch ends together and tuck under, forming a loaf about 7 inches long. Cover; let rise in a warm place till nearly double (about 30 minutes). Bake in a 375° oven for 15 to 20 minutes, covering with foil last 5 minutes of baking. Remove from tray; cool on wire rack. For icing combine powdered sugar, vanilla, and enough additional milk to make of drizzling consistency. Drizzle over loaf. Makes 1 loaf.

Cherry-Banana Loaf

⅓ cup sugar
3 tablespoons shortening
1 egg
¾ cup all-purpose flour
½ teaspoon baking soda
Dash salt
⅓ cup mashed banana (1 medium banana)
2 tablespoons milk
¼ cup drained maraschino cherries, quartered
3 tablespoons chopped walnuts

In small mixer bowl cream together the sugar and shortening till well blended. Add egg; beat well. Stir together all-purpose flour, baking soda, and salt. Combine the mashed banana and milk. Add the flour mixture to the creamed mixture alternately with the banana mixture, mixing well after each addition. Stir in the quartered maraschino cherries and chopped walnuts.

Turn the batter into 3 well-greased 4½x2½x1½-inch loaf pans. Bake in a 350° oven for 20 to 25 minutes or till bread tests done. Remove loaves from oven; let bread cool in the pans for 10 minutes. Remove loaves from pans and cool completely on a wire rack. Makes 3 loaves.

TOAST RINGS AND TOAST CUPS

Turn a bread slice into a toast ring or a toast cup to make creamed seafood or chicken à la king a noteworthy entrée.

For a toast ring, use two round cookie cutters, one 3-inch and one 2¼-inch, either scalloped or plain. Cut two circles of bread using the 3-inch cutter. With the small cutter, remove the center from one of the circles to form a ring. Spread the other bread circle with softened butter or margarine. Place the bread ring atop the circle. Bake in a 350° oven about 15 minutes.

For a toast cup, trim the crust from a slice of sandwich-style bread. Spread one side with softened butter or margarine. Carefully press into an ungreased muffin pan or 6-ounce custard cup, buttered side up. Bake in a 350° oven about 15 minutes.

Cocoa Crunch Ring

A quick and easy coffee cake that's extra special—

- 4 tablespoons butter *or* margarine, melted
- ⅓ cup finely chopped pecans
- ¼ cup presweetened cocoa powder
- 1 package (10) refrigerated biscuits
- ½ cup sifted powdered sugar (optional)
- 2 teaspoons milk (optional)

Pour *1 tablespoon* of the melted butter or margarine into a 3-cup oven-proof ring mold; lift and tilt mold to coat sides. Combine chopped pecans and presweetened cocoa powder; sprinkle *half* into the mold. Cut refrigerated biscuits into quarters. Dip biscuit quarters into the remaining 3 tablespoons melted butter.

Place *half* the biscuit quarters atop the nut layer. Sprinkle the remaining nut mixture atop, then place the remaining biscuit quarters atop nut layer. Bake in a 375° oven 20 to 25 minutes or till golden brown. Cool for 5 minutes in pan; invert pan onto a serving plate. If desired, combine powdered sugar with milk. Drizzle over warm coffee cake. Makes 1 coffee cake.

Mustard Buns

- 1¾ to 2 cups all-purpose flour
- 1 package active dry yeast
- ⅔ cup milk
- 2 tablespoons shortening
- 1 tablespoon sugar
- ½ teaspoon salt
- 1 egg
- ¼ cup cornmeal
- 2 tablespoons prepared mustard *or* horseradish mustard

In small mixer bowl combine ¾ cup of the flour and the yeast. In saucepan heat together milk, shortening, sugar, and salt just till warm (115° to 120°) and shortening almost melts, stirring constantly. Add to flour mixture; add egg, cornmeal, and mustard. Beat at low speed of electric mixer ½ minute, scraping sides of bowl constantly. Beat 3 minutes at high speed. Stir in as much of the remaining flour as you can mix in with a spoon. Turn out onto lightly floured surface. Knead in enough of the remaining flour to make a moderately stiff dough that is smooth and elastic (6 to 8 minutes total). Shape into a ball. Place in a greased bowl; turn once. Cover; let rise in warm place till double (30 to 45 minutes). Punch down; divide dough in half. Cover; let rest 10 minutes. Shape 1 portion at a time into 3 smooth balls; keep remaining dough in refrigerator till time to be shaped. Place on greased baking tray sprinkled with a little additional cornmeal. With palm of hand flatten balls to 4-inch circles. Cover and let rise till nearly double (about 30 minutes). Bake in a 375° oven about 15 minutes. remove from baking tray; cool on wire rack. Makes 6 buns.

Whole Wheat Bread

2½ to 3 cups whole wheat flour
1 package active dry yeast
1 cup milk
¼ cup honey
2 tablespoons cooking oil
1½ teaspoons salt

In mixer bowl combine 1½ cups of the whole wheat flour and the yeast. Heat together milk, honey, oil, and salt till just warm (115° to 120°); stir constantly. Add to flour mixture in mixer bowl. Beat at low speed of electric mixer for ½ minute, scraping sides of bowl. Beat 3 minutes at high speed. Stir in as much of the remaining whole wheat flour as you can with a spoon.

Turn out onto lightly floured surface; knead in enough of the remaining flour to make a moderately stiff dough that is smooth and elastic (6 to 8 minutes). Shape into a ball. Place in greased bowl, turning once to grease surface. Cover; let rise in warm place till double (about 1½ hours). Punch dough down; divide in half. Cover and let rest 10 minutes. Shape into 2 loaves.

Place in 2 greased 7½x3½x2-inch loaf pans. Cover; let rise till nearly double (about 45 minutes). Bake in a 350° oven for 35 to 40 minutes. Remove from pans. Cool on wire rack. Makes 2 loaves.

Rye-Kraut Bread

1½ to 1¾ cups all-purpose flour
1 package active dry yeast
1 to 2 teaspoons caraway seed
½ cup sauerkraut, rinsed, well-drained, and snipped
½ cup water
¼ cup packed brown sugar
1 tablespoon cooking oil
½ teaspoon salt
1 egg
1 cup rye flour
1 beaten egg yolk

In mixer bowl combine 1½ cups all-purpose flour, yeast, and caraway seed. Heat together the sauerkraut, water, brown sugar, oil and salt just till warm (115° to 120°); stir constantly. Add to flour mixture; add egg. Beat at low speed of electric mixer ½ minute, scraping bowl. Beat 3 minutes at high speed. Stir in rye flour and as much remaining all-purpose flour as you can mix in with a spoon.

Turn out onto lightly floured surface. Knead in enough remaining all-purpose flour to make a moderately stiff dough that is smooth and elastic (6 to 8 minutes total). Shape into a ball. Place in lightly greased bowl; turn once. Cover; let rise in warm place till double (about 1½ hours). Punch down. divide in half. Cover; let rest 10 minutes.

Shape into two 7- or 8-inch oblong loaves. Wrap, seal, label, and freeze 1 loaf. Place other loaf on greased baking tray. Cover; let rise till nearly double (about 40 minutes). Brush with mixture of beaten egg yolk and water. Bake in a 350° oven 40 to 45 minutes. Cool. To bake frozen loaf, thaw 1½ hours. Bake as above.

Orange Rolls

Also try cherry or boysenberry jam

- ¼ **cup orange marmalade**
- 1 **tablespoon butter** *or* **margarine, melted**
- ½ **package (1½ teaspoons) active dry yeast**
- ⅓ **cup warm water (110° to 115°)**
- 1 **cup packaged biscuit mix**
- ½ **teaspoon finely shredded orange** *or* **lemon peel**

Combine marmalade and melted butter or margarine. Spoon mixture into bottoms of 6 muffin pans. Set aside. Soften yeast in warm water. Add biscuit mix and shredded peel to yeast mixture, stirring till dry ingredients are moistened. By hand, beat about 20 strokes. Spoon batter atop marmalade mixture in muffin pans. Bake in a 375° oven 12 to 15 minutes. Loosen sides; invert onto serving plate. Makes 6 rolls.

Cheesy Noodles

- 1½ **cups medium noodles**
- ⅔ **cup cream-style cottage cheese with chives**
- 2 **tablespoons mayonnaise** *or* **salad dressing**
- ½ **cup shredded Swiss cheese (2 ounces)**
- 1 **tablespoon sesame seed, toasted**

Cook noodles according to package directions; drain. Combine noodles, cottage cheese, and mayonnaise or salad dressing. Turn noodle mixture into a greased 6½x6½x2-inch baking dish. Sprinkle with Swiss cheese and sesame seed. Bake in a 350° oven about 20 minutes or till heated through. Makes 2 servings.

Walnut Stuffing Balls

- ¼ **cup chopped onion**
- ¼ **cup chopped celery**
- 3 **tablespoons butter** *or* **margarine**
- 1 **beaten egg**
- ¼ **teaspoon salt**
- ¼ **teaspoon poultry seasoning**
- ⅛ **teaspoon pepper**
- 3 **slices whole wheat** *or* **white bread, cut into ¼-inch cubes (about 2 cups)**
- ½ **cup finely chopped walnuts**
- 2 **tablespoons finely snipped parsley**
- 2 **tablespoons toasted wheat germ**
- ¼ **teaspoon instant chicken bouillon granules**
- ¼ **cup hot water**

Cook onion and celery in butter or margarine till tender but not brown. Combine the beaten egg, salt, poultry seasoning, and pepper; stir in bread cubes, chopped walnuts, snipped parsley, wheat germ, and cooked onion mixture. Dissolve instant chicken bouillon granules in water. Add to bread mixture, tossing lightly to moisten. Using about ½ cup of the mixture for each, shape mixture into 4 balls. Place stuffing balls on greased baking tray. Bake in a 350° oven about 15 minutes or till heated through. Makes 4 servings.

Cheddar-Sauced Vegetables

½ pound fresh cauliflower, broccoli, *and/or* brussels sprouts
2 tablespoons finely chopped onion
1 tablespoon butter *or* margarine
1 tablespoon all-purpose flour
½ cup milk
¼ cup shredded cheddar cheese (1 ounce)
 Dash salt
 Dash pepper
2 tablespoons grated Parmesan cheese
 Paprika

Cut cauliflower into flowerets; cut off broccoli buds, and cut remaining part of spears into 1-inch pieces; halve large brussels sprouts (should have 2 cups total). Cook vegetables, covered, in small amount of boiling salted water about 10 minutes or till tender; drain. In small saucepan cook onion in the butter or margarine till tender but not brown. Stir in flour; add milk all at once. Cook and stir till thickened and bubbly. Stir in cheddar cheese; cook and stir till cheese melts. Season with salt and pepper. Pour some of the cheese mixture into a 2-cup casserole. Top with vegetable(s); pour remaining mixture over. Sprinkle with the Parmesan cheese and paprika. Bake in a 350° oven about 15 minutes or till heated through. Serve at once. Makes 3 servings.

Zucchini Parmigiana

1 small zucchini, thinly sliced (1 cup)
2 tablespoons grated Parmesan cheese
⅛ teaspoon dried basil, crushed
¼ cup pizza sauce
2 tablespoons shredded mozzarella cheese

In small plastic bag toss zucchini slices with Parmesan cheese and basil. Place in an 8- or 10-ounce casserole. Pour pizza sauce over. Bake, covered, in a 350° oven for 35 minutes. Uncover; sprinkle with mozzarella cheese. Return to oven; bake, uncovered, about 5 minutes or till cheese is melted. Makes 1 serving.

Wild Rice and Vegetable Bake

⅓ cup wild rice
1 small tomato, peeled, seeded, and chopped
¼ cup slivered almonds
3 tablespoons thinly sliced green onion
¾ cup chicken broth
½ cup chopped carrot
¼ teaspoon dried basil, crushed

Run cold water over rice in strainer about 1 minute, lifting rice to rinse well. In 1-quart casserole combine rice, tomato, almonds, and green onion. In small saucepan combine broth, carrot, and basil. Bring to boiling; reduce heat and simmer, covered, 5 minutes. Stir into mixture in casserole. Cover and bake in a 350° oven for 60 to 70 minutes or till rice is done. Makes 3 servings.

Herb-Stuffed Tomatoes

4 large tomatoes
1 cup herb-seasoned stuffing mix
2 tablespoons sliced green onion
2 tablespoons butter *or* margarine, melted
 Dash pepper
¼ cup grated Romano *or* Parmesan cheese

Slice a thin portion off the top of each tomato; discard tops. Scoop out the pulp from each tomato. Discard seeds; drain and chop tomato pulp. Cut a scalloped pattern around top edge of tomatoes, if desired. Invert the tomato shells on paper toweling to drain.

In a small bowl combine the chopped tomato pulp, herb-seasoned stuffing mix, sliced green onion, butter or margarine, and pepper. Lightly salt the tomato shells; fill with the stuffing mixture. Sprinkle with the grated Romano or Parmesan cheese. Place tomatoes on baking tray. Bake, uncovered, in a 375° oven about 20 minutes or till stuffing mixture is heated through and cheese is lightly browned. Garnish with parsley, if desired. Makes 4 servings.

Romaine Rice Rolls

4 large romaine leaves
½ cup cooked rice
½ cup shredded cucumber
¼ cup shredded carrot
2 tablespoons finely chopped onion
2 tablespoons mayonnaise *or* salad dressing
1 tablespoon plain yogurt
¼ teaspoon salt
¼ teaspoon dried dillweed
Dash pepper
1 tablespoon water

Immerse romaine leaves in boiling water for 2 to 3 minutes or just till limp; drain well. Remove stem end of heavy center vein from romaine leaves. Combine the cooked rice, shredded cucumber, shredded carrot, finely chopped onion, mayonnaise or salad dressing, yogurt, salt, dillweed, and pepper.

Place ¼ of the rice-vegetable mixture in the center of each romaine leaf. Fold in the sides of each leaf. Fold ends to overlap atop the rice-vegetable mixture. Place rolls, seam side down, in an 8x4x2-inch loaf pan. Pour 1 tablespoon water over the stuffed romaine rolls. Bake, covered, in a 350° oven about 20 minutes or till heated through. Makes 2 servings.

Romaine Rice Rolls
Cheesy Potato Boats
(see recipe, page 49)

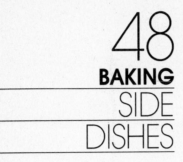

Bavarian Bean Bake

1 8-ounce can French-style
   green beans, drained
½ small apple, cored and
   sliced
Dash pepper
Caraway seed
1 teaspoon butter *or*
   margarine

In a 10-ounce baking dish combine beans, apple, and pepper. Sprinkle lightly with caraway seed. Dot with butter. Bake, covered, in a 375° oven for 25 to 30 minutes or till apple is tender. Makes 2 servings.

Corn-Filled Squash

1 small acorn squash (¾ to 1
   pound)
½ cup drained, canned whole
   kernel corn
1 tablespoon butter *or*
   margarine
2 tablespoons dairy sour
   cream
2 tablespoons cooked bacon
   pieces *or* 2 slices bacon,
   crisp-cooked, drained,
   and crumbled

Halve squash lengthwise; scoop out seeds. Place halves, cut side down, on baking tray. Bake in a 350° oven for 40 to 45 minutes or till tender. Turn squash cut side up; sprinkle with a little salt and pepper. Spoon corn into squash halves; dot with butter. Bake 5 to 10 minutes more or till heated through. Top with sour cream and bacon pieces. Makes 2 servings.

Baked Tomato-Asparagus Puffs

1 cup cut fresh asparagus
1 tablespoon butter *or*
   margarine
1 tablespoon all-purpose
   flour
⅓ cup vegetable juice
   cocktail
½ cup shredded cheddar
   cheese (2 ounces)
⅛ teaspoon salt
   Dash ground red pepper
2 beaten egg yolks
1 cup soft bread crumbs
   (about 1½ slices bread)
2 egg whites

In a 1-quart saucepan cook asparagus in butter or margarine over low heat 8 to 10 minutes or till tender. If desired, reserve several tips for garnish. Blend flour into cooked asparagus. Add vegetable juice cocktail all at once. Cook and stir till thickened and bubbly. Add cheese, salt, and red pepper, stirring till cheese is melted. Remove from heat. Gradually stir about *half* the hot mixture into egg yolks; return all to saucepan. Stir in bread crumbs. Beat egg whites till stiff peaks form; fold in cheese mixture. Pour into 4 ungreased 6-ounce custard cups. Place reserved asparagus tips atop. Bake, uncovered, in a 325° oven for 20 to 25 minutes or till a knife inserted halfway between center and edge comes out clean. Makes 4 servings.

HOW TO PREPARE CHEESY POTATO BOATS

Choose large baking potatoes and bake till tender. Cool the potatoes. To make potato boats, halve potatoes lengthwise and use a spoon to scoop out the inside, leaving a ¼-inch shell. Mash the scooped-out potato; beat in cottage cheese, French salad dressing, pimiento, and salt. Beat in some milk if necessary to make the potatoes fluffy.

For a decorative touch, pipe the mashed potato mixture into the potato shells. Fit a pastry or decorating bag with a star tip and then spoon the mashed potato mixture into the bag. Squeeze the bag gently but firmly to pipe the mixture into the shells. Or, simply spoon the mashed potato mixture into the shells.

Cheesy Potato Boats

Pictured on page 47 —

- **2 large baking potatoes**
- **¾ cup cream-style cottage cheese with chives**
- **2 teaspoons French salad dressing**
- **1 teaspoon chopped pimiento**
- **Milk**

Scrub potatoes; prick skins. Bake in a 425° oven about 1 hour and 10 minutes. Cut potatoes in half lengthwise; scoop out insides, leaving ¼-inch shells. Mash potato; beat in cottage cheese, dressing, pimiento, and ⅛ teaspoon *salt*. If necessary, beat in enough milk to make fluffy. Spoon or pipe into potato shells. Bake, covered, in a 350° oven for 25 to 30 minutes or till heated through. Serves 4.

Sweet Potato Puffs

- **1 8-ounce can sweet potatoes, drained**
- **1 tablespoon butter *or* margarine, softened**
- **Dash ground allspice**
- **1 tablespoon orange juice**
- **1 egg**
- **Butter *or* margarine, melted**

Mash sweet potatoes with a potato masher or on low speed of electric mixer. Add 1 tablespoon butter or margarine and allspice; mix well. Gradually mix in orange juice till potatoes are light and fluffy. Add egg; mix well. Spoon into 4 mounds on greased baking tray. Brush with melted butter or margarine. Bake in a 425° oven for 15 to 20 minutes. Makes 2 servings.

Orange Marbled Pound Cake

½ **cup butter** *or* **margarine**
2 **eggs**
¼ **cup milk**
1½ **cups all-purpose flour**
½ **teaspoon baking powder**
   Dash salt
¾ **cup sugar**
½ **teaspoon finely shredded orange peel**
2 **tablespoons orange juice**
2 **tablespoons chocolate-flavored syrup**

Bring butter or margarine, eggs, and milk to room temperature. Grease two 6x3x2-inch loaf pans; set aside. Stir together flour, baking powder, and salt.

In mixer bowl beat butter or margarine at medium speed with electric mixer till fluffy. Gradually add sugar, beating till light and fluffy. Add eggs, one at a time, beating at medium speed for 4 minutes after each addition; scrape bowl often. Add milk, orange peel, and orange juice; beat at low speed till blended. Gradually add dry ingredients to beaten mixture, beating at low speed just till smooth.

Divide batter in half. Stir chocolate-flavored syrup into half of the batter. In loaf pans alternate spoonfuls of light and dark batters. Using a narrow spatula, stir gently through batter to marble. Bake in a 325° oven about 45 minutes or till a wooden pick inserted in center comes out clean. Cool 10 minutes on wire rack. Remove cake loaves from pans; cool thoroughly. Makes 6 servings.

Carrot Cake Loaves

Pictured on pages 14 and 15—

⅓ **cup all-purpose flour**
2 **tablespoons toasted wheat germ**
¼ **teaspoon baking powder**
¼ **teaspoon baking soda**
¼ **teaspoon salt**
¼ **teaspoon ground cinnamon**
¼ **teaspoon ground nutmeg**
¼ **teaspoon finely shredded orange peel**
1 **beaten egg**
1 **medium carrot, finely shredded (½ cup)**
⅓ **cup sugar**
3 **tablespoons cooking oil**
   Cream Cheese Frosting *or* **canned creamy white frosting (optional)**
   Chopped walnuts (optional)

Grease and flour two 4½x 2½x1½-inch loaf pans; set aside. Stir together flour, wheat germ, baking powder, baking soda, salt, cinnamon, nutmeg, and shredded orange peel. Stir together the egg, shredded carrot, sugar, and cooking oil. Add the carrot mixture to dry ingredients; mix well.

Turn batter into the prepared loaf pans. Bake in a 350° oven about 20 minutes or till a wooden pick inserted in center comes out clean. Cool on wire rack for 10 minutes. Remove from pans; cool thoroughly on wire rack. If desired, frost sides and tops of cake loaves with Cream Cheese Frosting or canned frosting; sprinkle tops with chopped walnuts. Makes 4 servings.

Cream Cheese Frosting: In a small mixer bowl combine ½ of a 3-ounce package softened *cream cheese,* ¼ teaspoon *vanilla,* and dash *salt.* Beat till creamy. Gradually add ¾ to 1 cup sifted *powdered sugar,* beating till smooth and of spreading consistency.

Peach Upside-Down Cake

1 8¾-ounce can peach slices
1 tablespoon butter *or* margarine, melted
3 tablespoons brown sugar
¼ cup chopped nuts
3 tablespoons shortening
⅓ cup sugar
½ teaspoon vanilla
1 egg
¾ cup all-purpose flour
1¼ teaspoons baking powder
⅛ teaspoon salt

Drain peach slices, reserving the liquid. Pour melted butter into the bottom of an 8x6½x2-inch baking dish. Stir in brown sugar and *1 tablespoon* of the reserved peach liquid. If necessary, add water to remaining peach liquid to make ¼ cup; set aside. Arrange peach slices in baking dish; sprinkle with nuts. Bake in a 350° oven about 5 minutes or till peaches are hot.

Meanwhile, in a small mixer bowl beat shortening about 30 seconds. Add sugar and vanilla; beat till well combined. Add egg; beat 1 minute. Stir together flour, baking powder, and salt; add to shortening mixture alternately with the ¼ cup reserved peach liquid, beating after each addition. Spread batter atop the hot peach slices.

Bake in a 350° oven about 40 minutes or till a wooden pick inserted in the center of the cake comes out clean. Cool for 5 minutes on a wire rack; invert onto a serving plate. Serve warm. Makes 6 servings.

Cherry-Chocolate Nut Cupcakes

½ cup all-purpose flour
1 teaspoon baking powder
⅛ teaspoon salt
2 tablespoons butter *or* margarine
⅓ cup sugar
1 egg
1 square (1 ounce) unsweetened chocolate, melted and cooled
3 tablespoons dairy sour cream
¼ cup milk
2 tablespoons cherry preserves
2 tablespoons chopped walnuts

Stir together flour, baking powder, and salt. In mixer bowl beat butter or margarine about 30 seconds. Add sugar and beat till well combined. Add egg; beat 1 minute. Stir in cooled chocolate and sour cream.

Add dry ingredients and milk alternately to beaten mixture, beating at low speed with electric mixer after each addition just till combined. Cut up any large pieces of cherry preserves. Stir preserves and walnuts into batter.

Line muffin pan with paper bake cups; fill ¾ full. Bake in a 375° oven about 20 minutes or till a wooden pick inserted in center comes out clean. Cool on wire rack. Makes 6 cupcakes.

Banana Split Alaskas

You can substitute peppermint ice cream for the strawberry ice cream and sprinkle the sides with crushed peppermint candy—

1 doughnut, cut in half horizontally
½ banana, sliced
  Strawberry ice cream
  Chocolate-flavored syrup
2 tablespoons finely chopped pecans
2 egg whites
½ teaspoon vanilla
¼ teaspoon cream of tartar
¼ cup sugar
¼ cup finely chopped pecans *or* toasted coconut

Place doughnut halves, cut side up, on baking tray. Cover each half with banana slices, trimming slices even with doughnut edges if necessary. Top with a 1-inch layer of ice cream. Using a spoon, scoop out a shallow indentation in center of the ice cream. Fill indentations with some chocolate syrup and the 2 tablespoons chopped pecans. Place in freezer while preparing meringue.

For meringue, in a small mixer bowl beat egg whites, vanilla, and cream of tartar to soft peaks. Gradually add sugar, beating till stiff peaks form.

Remove doughnut halves from freezer. Quickly spread with meringue, sealing edges to baking tray all around. Swirl to make peaks. Sprinkle sides with ¼ cup chopped pecans or coconut. Cover loosely; freeze till firm. Bake, uncovered, in a 450° oven for 2 to 3 minutes or till meringue is lightly browned. Serve immediately. Serves 2.

Individual Peach Crisps

2 tablespoons sugar
1 tablespoon all-purpose flour
⅛ teaspoon ground cinnamon
2 cups sliced, peeled fresh peaches *or* one 16-ounce package frozen peach slices, thawed
1 tablespoonn grenadine syrup
2 teaspoons lemon juice
¼ cup quick-cooking rolled oats
¼ cup packed brown sugar
2 tablespoons all-purpose flour
2 tablespoons butter *or* margarine

In a medium mixing bowl combine sugar, 1 tablespoon flour, and cinnamon. Add fresh or thawed peach slices and toss till well coated. Carefully stir in grenadine syrup and lemon juice. Divide the peach mixture evenly among four 6-ounce custard cups or ramekins.

For crumb topper, in a small bowl combine quick-cooking rolled oats, brown sugar, and 2 tablespoons flour. Cut in the butter or margarine till mixture resembles coarse crumbs. Sprinkle crumb topper evenly over peach mixture in custard cups. Bake in a 375° oven about 30 minutes or till the crumb topping is golden brown. Serve warm. Makes 4 servings.

Fruit-Yogurt Shortcakes

The sour cream in the batter adds a distinctive flavor to these individual shortcakes—

½ cup packaged biscuit mix
2 teaspoons sugar
¼ cup dairy sour cream
2 teaspoons milk
1 cup assorted fresh fruit, drained canned fruit, *or* thawed frozen fruit
½ cup pineapple, lemon, *or* orange yogurt

Grease and flour the bottoms *only* of two 6½-ounce tuna cans; set aside. For shortcakes, stir together the packaged biscuit mix and sugar. Add sour cream and milk; stir just till moistened. Turn batter into prepared tuna cans. Bake in a 450° oven for 15 to 18 minutes or till golden brown. Cool in cans for 5 minutes. Remove shortcakes from cans.

Slice or cut up fruit as necessary. Stir yogurt till it reaches sauce consistency. Slice each shortcake in half horizontally. Place the bottom shortcake slices on serving plates. Add *half* of the fruit and *half* of the yogurt. Top with the remaining shortcake slices. Add the remaining fruit; drizzle with the remaining yogurt. Makes 2 servings.

**Fruit-Yogurt Shortcakes
Almond Cream Cones (see
recipe, page 55)**

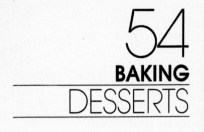

HOW TO MAKE ALMOND CREAM CONES

Drop level table-spoons of batter 3 to 3½ inches apart on the ungreased baking tray. These cookies spread, so be sure to drop only two cookies at a time on the tray. Bake the cookies in a 350° oven for 6 to 7 minutes.

Don't try to remove the baked cookies from the baking tray until they cool 1 to 2 minutes. Then remove the cookies using a wide metal spatula. If the cookies are difficult to remove from the tray, reheat them in the oven about 30 seconds.

Immediately roll each cookie into a cone. Grasp opposite sides and bring the edges together; overlap the edges to form a cone shape. Or, for uniform size, use a metal cone to shape the cookies. If cookies harden before rolling, reheat them in the oven about 30 seconds and then roll.

Almond Cream Cones

Pictured on page 53—

- 3 tablespoons brown sugar
- 2 tablespoons butter *or* margarine, melted
- 1 tablspoon dark corn syrup
- 1 teaspoon Amaretto
- ¼ cup all-purpose flour
- ⅛ teaspoon ground nutmeg
  Dash salt
- ½ cup whipping cream
- 1 tablespoon Amaretto
- 1 tablespoon chopped pistachio nuts *or* sliced almonds, toasted

In a small mixing bowl combine brown sugar, melted butter or margarine, corn syrup, and 1 teaspoon Amaretto; mix well. Stir together flour, nutmeg, and salt; stir into brown sugar mixture. Drop batter by level tablespoonfuls 3 to 3½ inches apart onto ungreased baking tray. (Bake only 2 cookies at a time; the batter will spread.) Bake the cookies in a 350° oven for 6 to 7 minutes.

Let cool for 1 to 2 minutes. *While cookies are still warm* remove one at a time with a wide metal spatula and immediately roll each to form a cone. (For uniform size, use a metal cone for shaping.) If cookies cool and become hard before they are shaped, reheat in the oven about 30 seconds. Place cookies, seam side down, on a wire rack; cool thoroughly. Store in an airtight container.

Just before serving, beat whipping cream and 1 tablespoon Amaretto till soft peaks form. Pipe or spoon whipped cream mixture into each cone. Sprinkle whipped cream with pistachio nuts or almonds. Serve immediately. Makes 6 cones.

Orange Meringue Rice Pudding

- 2 cups milk
- ⅓ cup long grain rice
- 2 beaten egg yolks
- 2 tablespoons orange marmalade
- ½ teaspoon vanilla
  Dash salt
- 2 egg whites
- 3 tablespoons sugar

In a heavy saucepan combine milk and rice. Bring to boiling; reduce heat. Cover and cook over low heat about 15 minutes or till rice is tender. Remove from heat.

Gradually stir about *1 cup* of the hot rice mixture into beaten egg yolks. Return all to saucepan. Stir in orange marmalade, vanilla, and salt. Pour rice mixture into an 8x6½x2-inch baking dish. Bake, uncovered, in a 350° oven for 12 minutes. Remove from oven. Stir rice mixture well.

For meringue, beat egg whites till soft peaks form. Gradually add sugar, beating till stiff peaks form. Spread meringue evenly over the rice mixture, sealing to edges of baking dish. Swirl to make decorative peaks. Return to 350° oven; bake for 8 to 10 minutes more or till the meringue is golden brown. Serve the pudding warm or cool in individual dessert dishes. Makes 6 servings.

Whole Wheat Turnovers

- ¼ cup flaked coconut
- ¼ cup raisins
- ¼ cup apricot preserves
- 2 tablespoons chopped pecans
- 1 teaspoon lemon juice
- ¾ cup whole wheat flour
- 2 teaspoons brown sugar
- ⅛ teaspoon salt
- ¼ cup butter *or* margarine
- ¼ cup dairy sour cream
- ¼ cup sifted powdered sugar
  Dash vanilla
  Milk

In a mixing bowl combine flaked coconut, raisins, apricot preserves, pecans, and lemon juice; set aside. Stir together whole wheat flour, brown sugar, and salt. Cut in butter or margarine till mixture resembles coarse crumbs. Stir in the sour cream; mix till the mixture forms a ball.

Divide dough into 5 portions. On a lightly floured surface roll each portion into a 4½-inch circle. Place 1 rounded tablespoonful of the coconut mixture atop each circle. Fold one side of dough over mixture; seal edges by pressing with tines of a fork. Place on ungreased baking tray.

Bake in a 375° oven for 20 to 25 minutes or till lightly browned. Cool slightly on a wire rack. Combine powdered sugar, vanilla, and enough milk to make of drizzling consistency. Drizzle over warm turnovers. Makes 5 turnovers.

SHAPE YOUR OWN TART SHELLS

For easy, dressed-up desserts, make your own tart shells. Prepare Tart and Pie Pastry (see recipe at right). On a lightly floured surface roll out the pastry to ⅛-inch thickness. Cut into three 4½-inch circles or squares. Fit the dough circles or squares over inverted muffin pans or 6-ounce custard cups, pinching pleats at intervals to fit around the pans. Prick pastry with a fork. (If using custard cups, place on baking tray.) Bake in a 450° oven for 7 to 10 minutes or till tart shells are golden. Cool on a wire rack. Fill baked tart shells with pudding, pie filling, or fruit and top with sweetened whipped cream or frozen whipped dessert topping, thawed.

TWO WAYS TO SHAPE TART SHELLS

Shape tart shells over muffin pans or 6-ounce custard cups. First prepare Tart and Pie Pastry and roll it out to ⅛-inch thickness. Cut the pastry into three 4½-inch circles or squares. When using muffin pans, place a pastry circle or square over the inverted pan. Gently mold the pastry over the pan and then pinch the pastry into pleats to fit the pan.

When using custard cups, position and pleat the pastry in the same manner. Place the custard cups on the baking tray before baking.

Tart and Pie Pastry

½ cup all-purpose flour
¼ teaspoon salt
3 tablespoons shortening
1 tablespoon cold water

In a small mixing bowl stir together the flour and salt; cut in shortening till pieces are the size of small peas. Sprinkle the water over mixture. Gently toss with a fork and push moistened part to one side. Repeat if necessary, tossing the mixture with *1 to 2 teaspoons* more water to moisten.

Gather up mixture with fingers; form into 2 balls. On a lightly floured surface, flatten each ball slightly; roll into a 7-inch circle. If edges split, pinch together. Roll up one of the pastry circles on rolling pin; unroll over one 4½x1-inch pie plate, fitting loosely onto bottom and sides. Trim to ½ inch beyond edge of pie plate. Turn under and flute edge. Repeat with the remaining pastry circle.

For a baked pastry shell, prick bottom and sides with tines of a fork. Bake in a 450° oven for 10 to 12 minutes or till golden brown. For an unbaked pastry shell, do not prick. Add the desired filling and bake as directed in the recipe. Makes two 4-inch pastry shells.

Whole Wheat Tart and Pie Pastry: Prepare Tart and Pie Pastry as above, *except* substitute ¼ cup *whole wheat flour* and ¼ cup *all-purpose flour* for the ½ cup all-purpose flour.

Apple Crumble Pies for Two

Tart and Pie Pastry (see recipe at left)
1 tablespoon sugar
1 tablespoon brown sugar
¼ teaspoon ground cinnamon
2 cups thinly sliced, peeled cooking apples
2 tablespoons sugar
2 tablespoons all-purpose flour
⅛ teaspoon ground nutmeg
Dash ground ginger
1 tablespoon butter *or* margarine

Prepare and roll out pastry; line two 4½x1-inch pie plates. Trim pastry to ½ inch beyond edge of pie plate. Flute edge; do not prick. In a small bowl stir together the 1 tablespoon sugar, brown sugar, and cinnamon. Toss sliced apples with the sugar mixture to coat. Divide apple mixture evenly between the two pastry shells.

Combine the 2 tablespoons sugar, flour, nutmeg, and ginger. Cut in the butter or margarine till crumbly; sprinkle atop the apple mixture. To prevent overbrowning, cover edges of pies with foil. Bake in a 375° oven for 20 minutes. Remove foil; bake about 25 minutes more or till topping is golden brown. Serve pies warm with vanilla ice cream or sliced cheddar or American cheese, if desired. Makes two 4-inch pies.

Chocolate-Rum Refrigerator Cookies

¾ **cup all-purpose flour**
¼ **teaspoon baking soda**
¼ **teaspoon salt**
½ **cup sifted powdered sugar**
3 **tablespoons butter** *or* **margarine**
1 **egg**
½ **teaspoon rum flavoring**
1 **square (1 ounce) unsweetened chocolate, melted and cooled**
¼ **cup finely chopped walnuts**

In a small bowl stir together flour, baking soda, and salt. In a small mixer bowl beat powdered sugar and butter or margarine till well blended. Add egg and rum flavoring; beat well. Stir in unsweetened chocolate. Add dry ingredients to beaten mixture; beat just till well blended. Stir in finely chopped nuts. Cover and chill about 30 minutes. Shape into a 7-inch-long roll. Wrap in waxed paper or clear plastic wrap; chill several hours or overnight.

Cut desired amount of cookie dough into ¼-inch slices; place 1 inch apart on greased baking tray. Rewrap and chill remaining dough. Bake cookie slices in a 375° oven for 6 to 8 minutes or till done. Cool about 1 minute; remove to a wire rack. Cool. Makes about 24.

Oatmeal Chippers

¾ **cup all-purpose flour**
½ **teaspoon baking soda**
⅓ **cup butter** *or* **margarine**
¼ **cup peanut butter**
1 **cup packed brown sugar**
1 **egg**
½ **teaspoon vanilla**
1½ **cups quick-cooking rolled oats**
½ **cup semisweet chocolate pieces**

Mix flour and soda. Beat butter and peanut butter with electric mixer 30 seconds. Add sugar; beat till fluffy. Add egg and vanilla; beat well. Add dry ingredients; beat well. Stir in oats and chocolate.

Drop from teaspoon 2 inches apart onto ungreased baking tray. Bake in 375° oven 8 to 10 minutes. Remove; cool on wire rack. Makes about 36.

Anise Sugar Cookies

1¾ **cups all-purpose flour**
1 **teaspoon whole anise seed**
½ **teaspoon baking soda**
⅓ **cup butter** *or* **margarine**
1 **cup sugar**
1 **egg**
1 **teaspoon vanilla**
⅓ **cup milk**

Stir together flour, anise seed, soda, and ½ teaspoon *salt*. Beat butter 30 seconds. Add sugar; beat till fluffy. Add egg and vanilla; beat well. Blend in milk. Add dry ingredients; beat well.

Drop from a teaspoon 2 inches apart onto ungreased baking tray. Bake in 375° oven 7 to 8 minutes. Cool 1 minute; remove to wire rack. Cool. Makes about 30.

Pecan-Coconut Bars

¾ cup all-purpose flour
1 tablespoon sugar
3 tablespoons butter *or* margarine
1 egg
¼ cup packed brown sugar
¼ cup chopped pecans *or* walnuts
¼ cup flaked *or* shredded coconut
¼ cup light corn syrup
2 tablespoons butter *or* margarine, melted
½ teaspoon vanilla

In a mixing bowl stir together the all-purpose flour and sugar; cut in the 3 tablespoons butter or margarine. Pat flour mixture into the bottom of an ungreased 8x6½x2-inch baking dish. Bake in a 350° oven for 20 minutes.

Meanwhile, in a mixing bowl beat the egg slightly; stir in the brown sugar, chopped pecans or walnuts, flaked or shredded coconut, light corn syrup, 2 tablespoons melted butter or margarine, and the vanilla. Pour the coconut-pecan mixture over the baked layer. Return to 350° oven; bake about 30 minutes or till the coconut layer is done. Cool slightly on a wire rack; cut into bars. Makes 12 bars.

Dried Fruit Bars

2 tablespoons brown sugar
2 tablespoons butter *or* margarine, softened
⅔ cup quick-cooking rolled oats
2 tablespoons whole wheat flour
½ cup finely snipped mixed dried fruits
¼ cup boiling water
1 tablespoon butter *or* margarine
1 slightly beaten egg
3 tablespoons brown sugar
3 tablespoons whole wheat flour
1 tablespoon toasted wheat germ
¼ teaspoon salt
¼ teaspoon ground cinnamon
Dash ground cloves
¼ cup chopped walnuts

In a bowl stir together the 2 tablespoons brown sugar and the 2 tablespoons softened butter or margarine. Stir in rolled oats and the 2 tablespoons whole wheat flour. Reserve ¼ cup of the oat mixture. Press the remaining oat mixture into the bottom of a greased 8x6½x2-inch baking dish. Bake in a 350° oven for 10 minutes.

Meanwhile, combine dried fruit, boiling water, and 1 tablespoon butter or margarine; let stand for 5 minutes. Stir in egg, 3 tablespoons brown sugar, 3 tablespoons whole wheat flour, wheat germ, salt, cinnamon, and cloves. Stir in walnuts. Spread fruit mixture over the baked layer. Top with the reserved ¼ cup oat mixture. Return to 350° oven; bake for 25 to 30 minutes or till done. Cool slightly on a wire rack; cut into bars. Makes 16 bars.

Frosted Coffee-Spice Bars

½ cup all-purpose flour
¼ teaspoon baking soda
¼ teaspoon ground cinnamon
⅛ teaspoon ground nutmeg
⅛ teaspoon ground allspice
Dash salt
¼ cup raisins
¼ cup strong coffee
2 tablespoons shortening *or* cooking oil
1 egg
¼ cup sugar
2 tablespoons chopped walnuts
¾ cup sifted powdered sugar
2 tablespoons butter *or* margarine
1 tablespoon strong coffee

Stir together flour, baking soda, cinnamon, nutmeg, allspice, and salt. In a saucepan combine raisins and ¼ cup strong coffee; bring to boiling. Remove from heat. Stir in shortening or cooking oil; cool to lukewarm. Combine egg, sugar, and raisin mixture; beat well. Add dry ingredients to raisin mixture and beat till blended. Stir in nuts. Turn into a greased 8x6½x2-inch baking dish. Bake in a 375° oven about 15 minutes or till done. Cool on a wire rack.

For frosting, in a small mixer bowl beat *half* of the powdered sugar and the butter or margarine with an electric mixer. Beat in 1 tablespoon strong coffee. Gradually beat in the remaining powdered sugar. If necessary, add additional strong coffee to make frosting of spreading consistency. Frost cookies; cut into bars. Makes 12.

BROILING

It's hard to believe these taste-tempting specialties were broiled in a toaster oven. The *Broiler Torte, Broiler Salmon Steaks, Chinese Chicken Wings,* and *Appetizer Cheese Melt* are all proof that toaster oven broiling isn't limited to steaks and chops (see index for recipe pages). So try some of the sure-to-please hors d'oeuvres and first-class main dishes. And don't forget the vegetables, the hot, crunchy breads, or the desserts.

Chinese Chicken Wings

Pictured on pages 60 and 61 —

- ¼ **cup beer**
- 3 **tablespoons hoison sauce**
- 1 **tablespoon apple jelly**
- ¼ **teaspoon five-spice powder**
- 8 **chicken wings, tips removed and cut at joints**

In small saucepan combine the beer, hoison sauce, apple jelly, and five-spice powder. Cook and stir till heated through. Place chicken wings on rack of unheated broiler pan. Broil chicken for 10 minutes. Brush with some of the sauce. Turn chicken. Broil about 10 minutes more, brushing occasionally with sauce. To serve, pass remaining sauce. Makes 3 appetizers.

Burger Reubens

- ¼ **pound ground beef**
- 2 **tablespoons finely chopped onion**
- ½ **cup sauerkraut, drained**
- ¼ **teaspoon celery seed**
- 4 **slices rye bread** *or* **pumpernickel bread**
  Russian salad dressing
- ½ **cup shredded Swiss cheese**

In skillet cook ground beef and onion till beef is brown and onion is tender. Drain well. Stir in sauerkraut and celery seed. Heat through. Toast bread; spread lightly with salad dressing. Top each slice with ¼ of the ground beef mixture. Sprinkle each with about 2 tablespoons of the shredded Swiss cheese. Broil about 3 minutes or till cheese melts. To serve, cut each bread slice into 6 portions. Serve hot. Makes 24 appetizers.

Appetizer Cheese Melt

Pictured on pages 60 and 61—

- 1 **8-ounce package Monterey Jack cheese with jalapeño peppers, shredded**
- ½ **cup shredded American cheese**
- 8 **slices bacon, crisp-cooked, drained and crumbled**
- ¼ **cup milk**
  Tortilla chips
  Assorted fresh vegetables such as halved radishes, sliced zucchini, and celery
  Hot cooked cauliflower flowerets *and/or* **hot cooked new potatoes, halved**

In small mixer bowl combine Monterey Jack cheese, American cheese, and bacon. Heat milk to boiling; pour over cheeses. Beat with electric mixer till nearly smooth. Form mixture into a circle 4½ inches in diameter. Cover and chill several hours or overnight.

Place cheese circle on oven-going plate; broil 3 to 4 minutes or till cheese melts on surface. To serve, scrape off melted portion and spread on tortilla chips or vegetables. Continue returning to broiler and repeating the melting and scraping process till all cheese is melted. Makes 1½ cups.

Pumpernickel Egg Puffs

16 slices party pumpernickel
   bread *or* party rye bread
¼ cup cheese spread *or*
   Swiss-flavored cheese
   spread
 2 egg yolks
 1 tablespoon milk
½ of a 2½-ounce package
   very thinly sliced smoked
   beef, finely chopped
 1 tablespoon chopped
   pimiento
 1 tablespoon chopped green
   pepper (optional)
 1 teaspoon butter *or*
   margarine
 2 egg whites

Toast bread slices. Spread
with cheese spread almost to edges
of bread. In a small mixing bowl
beat together the egg yolks and
milk; stir in the smoked beef, pimiento, and green pepper. In a
small skillet melt the butter or margarine over medium heat. Pour in
the egg yolk mixture. Cook without
stirring till mixture begins to set on
the bottom and around edges. Remove from heat.

Beat egg whites till frothy. Fold
partially cooked egg yolk mixture
into egg whites. Place bread slices
on rack of unheated broiler pan.
Place about 1 tablespoon of the
egg mixture atop cheese spread
on each slice of bread. Broil for 3
to 4 minutes or till lightly browned.
Makes 16 appetizers.

HOW TO MAKE PUMPER-NICKEL EGG PUFFS

Spread cheese
spread on toasted
bread slices. Cover
each slice gener-
ously and be sure to
spread almost to the
edges. Vary the fla-
vor of these tasty
appetizers by using
your choice of party
pumpernickel or
party rye bread and
regular or Swiss-fla-
vored cheese
spread.

Top each bread
slice with about 1 ta-
blespoon of the egg
topping mixture. To
make the egg top-
ping, combine egg
yolks, milk, finely
chopped smoked
beef, pimiento, and
green pepper. Cook
this mixture and then
fold it into the
beaten egg whites.

As the appetizers
broil, the egg top-
ping puffs and
browns. Remove the
hot puffs from the
pan with a metal
spatula. Serve the
appetizers warm.

Savory Swiss Burgers

1 beaten egg
¼ cup finely chopped onion
2 tablespoons toasted wheat germ
2 tablespoons milk
½ teaspoon salt
½ teaspoon dried savory, crushed
⅛ teaspoon pepper
¾ pound ground beef
2 slices Swiss cheese, halved diagonally (2 ounces)
4 tomato slices
4 kaiser rolls *or* hamburger buns, split and toasted
Watercress (optional)

In mixing bowl combine beaten egg, chopped onion, wheat germ, milk, salt, savory, and pepper. Add ground beef; mix well. Shape into four patties ½ inch thick.

Place patties on rack of unheated broiler pan. Broil till desired doneness, turning once (allow about 8 minutes total time for rare; about 10 minutes for medium; and about 12 minutes for well-done). During last minute of broiling time, place cheese slices and tomato slices atop burgers. Serve burgers in toasted rolls or hamburger buns. Add watercress, if desired. Makes 4 servings.

Pita Burgers

1 pound ground beef
¼ cup taco sauce
½ teaspoon garlic salt
1 16-ounce can refried beans
5 halves of large pita bread rounds
Shredded lettuce
1 avocado, seeded, peeled, and sliced

Mix beef, taco sauce, and garlic salt. Shape into five 3½-inch-diameter patties; place on rack of unheated broiler pan. Broil to desired doneness, turning once (allow about 8 minutes total for medium). Spread beans inside bread rounds. Insert burgers into bread. Top with lettuce and avocado. Pass more taco sauce, if desired. Makes 5 servings.

Poor Boy Filets

6 slices bacon
1 2-ounce can chopped mushrooms, drained
¼ cup grated Parmesan cheese
3 tablespoons finely chopped pimiento-stuffed olives
2 tablespoons finely chopped onion
2 tablespoons finely chopped green pepper
¼ teaspoon lemon pepper
1 pound ground beef

Partially cook bacon; drain well and set aside. Combine mushrooms, cheese, olives, onion, green pepper, and lemon pepper. Add beef; mix well. Shape into six 2½-inch-diameter patties. Wrap 1 bacon slice around each patty; secure with wooden picks. Place on rack of unheated broiler pan. Broil to desired doneness, turning once (allow 12 to 14 minutes total time for medium). Serves 6.

Sunday Evening Stack-Ups

Mayonnaise *or* salad
   dressing
4 hamburger buns, split and
   toasted
1 beaten egg
⅓ cup soft bread crumbs
¼ teaspoon salt
½ pound ground beef
2 eggs
2 tablespoons milk
⅛ teaspoon salt
1 tablespoon butter *or*
   margarine
4 slices American cheese
4 lettuce leaves
½ avocado, seeded, peeled,
   and cut into 8 slices

Spread mayonnaise on cut surfaces of buns; set aside. In bowl combine the 1 egg, the bread crumbs, and the ¼ teaspoon salt. Add ground beef; mix well. Shape meat mixture into 4 patties 4½ to 5 inches in diameter. Broil 3 to 4 minutes on each side for medium doneness.

Meanwhile, beat together the remaining eggs, milk and the ⅛ teaspoon salt. In skillet cook the egg mixture in butter or margarine just till set. Place cheese slices atop burgers; return to oven. Broil burgers about 1 minute or till the cheese is melted.

Place lettuce and cheese-topped patty on bottom half of buns; top each with spoonful of egg mixture and 2 avocado slices. Cover with bun top. Makes 4 servings.

BROILING CHART

Note: Broil all foods at lowest setting of broiling rack.

Food/Amount	Total Time (minutes)
Beef steak, ¾ inch thick	
rare	6 to 8
medium	10 to 12
well-done	14 to 16
Beef steak, 1 inch thick	
rare	8 to 10
medium	12 to 14
well-done	18 to 20
Hamburgers, ½ inch thick	
rare	about 8
medium	about 10
well-done	about 12
Lamb chops, ¾ inch thick	
medium	10 to 12
well-done	14 to 16
Pork chops, ½ to ¾ inch thick	15 to 20
Pork chops *or* pork steaks, ¾ to 1 inch thick	20 to 25
Fully cooked ham center slice, 1 inch thick	12 to 14
Bacon	5 to 6
Canadian-style bacon slices	2 to 4
Frankfurters	about 6
Link sausage	
fully cooked	5 to 6
uncooked	about 10
Chicken pieces	20 to 30
Fish fillets *or* steaks, ½ to ¾ inch thick	
fresh	about 5
frozen	10 to 12
Fish fillets *or* steaks, 1 inch thick	
fresh	about 10
frozen	about 18
Scallops	about 3
Shrimp	about 3

Place on rack of unheated broiler pan. Broil on one side for half the time indicated in the chart for desired doneness. Turn; broil for remaining time. *Exception:* Fish fillets or fish steaks less than 1 inch thick should be broiled on only one side for entire time.

**Broiled Beef Steak with
Sherry Sauce**

Broiled Beef Steak with Sherry Sauce

1½ pounds beef T-bone steak, cut 1 inch thick, *or* 1 pound beef top loin steak, cut 1 inch thick
1 small onion, thinly sliced and separated into rings
¼ teaspoon curry powder
1 clove garlic, minced
1 tablespoon butter *or* margarine
2 teaspoons cornstarch
¼ teaspoon sugar
¼ teaspoon instant beef bouillon granules
⅛ teaspoon ground ginger
¼ cup water
3 tablespoons dry sherry
1 small tomato, peeled, seeded, and chopped
1 tablespoon snipped parsley

Trim excess fat from steak; sprinkle with salt and pepper. Place steak on rack of unheated broiler pan. Broil to desired doneness, turning steak once (allow 12 to 14 minutes total broiling time for medium).

Meanwhile, in small saucepan cook onion, curry powder, and garlic in butter or margarine till onion is tender but not brown. Blend in cornstarch, sugar, beef bouillon granules, and ginger. Add water and sherry; cook and stir till thickened and bubbly. Cook and stir 2 minutes more. Stir in tomato and snipped parsley; heat through. Spoon over meat. If desired, garnish with parsley sprigs and sautéed fluted mushrooms. Makes 4 servings.

Sesame Broiled Steak

1 pound beef top round steak, cut ¾-inch thick
½ teaspoon unseasoned meat tenderizer
3 tablespoons soy sauce
1 tablespoon cooking oil
1 tablespoon lemon juice
1 tablespoon water
Several drops bottled hot pepper sauce
2 tablespoons honey
1 8¼-ounce can pineapple slices, drained
1 tablespoon sesame seed, toasted

Sprinkle both sides of meat with tenderizer. To ensure penetration, pierce deeply at ½-inch intervals with a long-tined fork.

For marinade combine soy sauce, cooking oil, lemon juice, water, and hot pepper sauce. Place meat in shallow pan. Pour marinade over meat. Cover and refrigerate for 1 to 2 hours, turning meat once or twice. Drain meat, reserving marinade.

Place meat on rack of unheated broiler pan. Broil for 10 minutes, turning once and brushing with marinade. Meanwhile, combine remaining marinade and honey. Arrange pineapple slices atop meat; brush meat and pineapple with honey mixture. Return to oven; broil 2 to 3 minutes more for medium doneness. Brush any remaining honey mixture over all. Sprinkle with sesame seed. Makes 4 servings.

Sweet and Sour Pork Chops with Raisin Sauce

2 pork loin rib chops, cut 1
  inch thick
1 tablespoon brown sugar
1 teaspoon cornstarch
⅛ teaspoon ground ginger
½ cup unsweetened
  pineapple juice
1 tablespoon vinegar
1 teaspoon soy sauce
2 tablespoons raisins
2 tablespoons thinly sliced
  green onion
2 tablespoons chopped
  green pepper
  Hot cooked rice

Place pork chops on rack of unheated broiler pan. Sprinkle chops lightly with salt and pepper, if desired. Broil chops till done, turning once (allow 25 to 30 minutes total time).

Meanwhile, prepare sauce. In small saucepan combine brown sugar, cornstarch, and ginger. Stir in pineapple juice, vinegar, and soy sauce. Add raisins, thinly sliced green onion, and green pepper.

Cook and stir till thickened and bubbly. Cook and stir 2 minutes more. Arrange pork chops over cooked rice; spoon sauce atop. Makes 2 servings.

Moroccan-Style Chops

3 tablespoons plain yogurt
2 tablespoons orange juice
1 tablespoon sliced green
  onion
¼ teaspoon salt
¼ teaspoon ground coriander
⅛ teaspoon ground cumin
⅛ teaspoon ground cinnamon
⅛ teaspoon ground turmeric
  Dash ground cloves
3 pork loin rib chops, cut ¾
  inch thick
1 small onion, chopped
½ medium tomato, seeded
  and chopped
½ medium cucumber, seeded
  and chopped
¼ cup plain yogurt
  Hot cooked couscous or
  rice (optional)
  Quartered orange slices
  (optional)

For marinade, in a small bowl combine the 3 tablespoons, yogurt, the orange juice, green onion, salt, coriander; cumin, cinnamon, turmeric, and cloves. Arrange chops in a shallow dish. Pour marinade over chops. Cover; marinate in refrigerator overnight, turning chops occasionally. Remove chops from marinade, scraping off as much marinade as possible. Reserve marinade.

In mixing bowl combine chopped onion, tomato, and cucumber; stir in the ¼ cup yogurt. Chill. Place chops on rack of unheated broiler pan. Broil for 10 minutes. Turn chops; broil 10 to 15 minutes more or till done, brushing often with marinade. Keep marinade warm; do not boil.

To serve, transfer chops to platter atop couscous or rice, if desired. Spoon some of the marinade over each chop. Serve with yogurt-vegetable mixture; pass the oranges if desired. Makes 3 servings.

Barbecue Pork Ribs

Country-style ribs are the meatiest of all pork ribs—

- **2 pounds pork country-style ribs**
- **¼ cup catsup**
- **1 tablespoon finely chopped onion**
- **1 tablespoon cooking oil**
- **1 teaspoon Worcestershire sauce**
- **¼ teaspoon prepared mustard**
  Several dashes bottled hot pepper sauce
  Dash ground cloves

Cut pork ribs into serving-size pieces. In medium saucepan pour enough water over the ribs to cover completely. Bring water to boiling; reduce heat. Cover the saucepan and simmer about 45 minutes or till ribs are nearly tender. Drain on paper toweling.

For barbecue sauce, in small saucepan combine the catsup, onion, cooking oil, Worcestershire sauce, prepared mustard, hot pepper sauce, and cloves. Bring to boiling. Place ribs on rack of unheated broiler pan. Broil ribs for 10 minutes; brush with barbecue sauce. Turn ribs. Broil about 10 minutes more, brushing occasionally with the barbecue sauce till ribs are well glazed. Makes 4 servings.

Pork Kabobs Glazed with Applesauce

Pork, carrots, and beets are combined in this colorful entrée—

- **1 large carrot, cut into 1-inch pieces**
- **½ pound boneless pork, cut into 1-inch cubes**
- **¼ cup applesauce**
- **¼ cup bottled barbecue sauce**
- **1 tablespoon vinegar**
- **⅛ teaspoon ground allspice**
- **½ of an 8-ounce can tiny whole beets**

Cook carrot pieces in small amount of boiling salted water for about 15 minutes or till nearly tender; drain well. On 4 skewers alternately thread the pork cubes and carrot pieces.

For sauce in a small bowl combine the applesauce, the barbecue sauce, the vinegar, and the allspice. Place the kabobs on rack of unheated broiler pan. Broil kabobs for 8 to 10 minutes. Brush with the sauce; turn kabobs. Add the tiny whole beets to the kabobs. Broil for 8 to 10 minutes more or till the pork is done. Brush kabobs again with the sauce just before serving. Makes 2 servings.

Canadian Bacon Stack-Up

Make this easy open-faced sandwich when you want a quick, hot meal for two—

- **⅓ cup shredded cheddar, Swiss, *or* Monterey Jack cheese**
- **½ small tomato, peeled, seeded, and chopped (about ¼ cup)**
- **¼ cup chopped cucumber**
- **1 tablespoon mayonnaise *or* salad dressing**
  Dash ground coriander
- **2 slices Canadian-style bacon, cut ½-inch thick (4 ounces)**
- **1 English muffin, split and toasted**

In a small bowl stir together the shredded cheddar, Swiss, or Monterey Jack cheese, chopped tomato, chopped cucumber, mayonnaise or salad dressing, and coriander; set aside. Slash the edges of the Canadian-style bacon slices. Place bacon slices on rack of unheated broiler pan. Broil for 1 to 2 minutes on each side.

Place 1 bacon slice atop each toasted English muffin half. Spread cheese mixture evenly atop each Canadian bacon slice. Place sandwich halves on rack of broiler pan. Broil sandwich halves for 2 to 3 minutes or till cheese is melted. Makes 2 servings.

Fruit-Topped Ham Slice

1 ¾-pound fully cooked ham
    slice, cut 1 inch thick
½ of an 8½-ounce can
    pineapple slices
2 tablespoons orange
    marmalade
    Dash ground cloves

Slash fat edge of ham slice. Place on rack of unheated broiler pan. Broil for 7 to 8 minutes. Turn; broil 5 to 6 minutes more. Meanwhile, drain the pineapple slices, reserving 2 tablespoons of the liquid. Combine the reserved pineapple liquid, orange marmalade, and cloves. Place pineapple slices atop ham slice. Spoon marmalade mixture over ham. Broil for 2 to 3 minutes more or till marmalade mixture and fruit are heated through. Makes 2 or 3 servings.

Sesame Chicken Drumsticks

2 tablespoons soy sauce
1 tablespoon cooking oil
¼ teaspoon onion powder
    Dash pepper
4 chicken drumsticks (about
    1 pound total)
¼ cup sesame seed, toasted

Combine soy sauce, cooking oil, onion powder, and pepper. Brush chicken drumsticks with soy sauce mixture. Roll chicken drumsticks in toasted sesame seed to coat. Place chicken on rack of unheated broiler pan. Broil about 30 minutes or till done, turning once. Makes 2 servings.

Tangy Chicken Rolls

2 whole medium chicken
    breasts, skinned, halved
    lengthwise, and boned
½ of a 3-ounce package
    cream cheese, softened
1½ teaspoons prepared
    mustard
½ teaspoon onion powder
2 tablespoons butter *or*
    margarine, melted
¼ cup crushed whole wheat
    crackers

Place chicken breasts, bone side up, between 2 pieces of clear plastic wrap. Pound out from center with meat mallet to ⅛-inch thickness. Remove plastic wrap; season both sides of chicken with salt and pepper.

Combine softened cream cheese, mustard, and onion powder. Spread about 1 tablespoon of the cream cheese mixture on 1 side of each chicken breast. Fold in sides and roll up jelly-roll style. (Be sure the folded sides are inside the roll.) Secure with wooden picks.

Place chicken rolls on rack of unheated broiler pan. Brush with some of the butter or margarine. Broil about 10 minutes. Turn and brush with butter; broil about 10 minutes longer or till done. Top with crushed crackers just before serving. Makes 4 servings.

Chicken Breasts with Dilled Mushroom Sauce

2 whole medium chicken breasts, skinned, halved lengthwise, and boned
Butter *or* margarine, melted
2 tablespoons thinly sliced green onion
1 tablespoon butter *or* margarine, melted
2 teaspoons all-purpose flour
1 2½-ounce jar sliced mushrooms, drained
¼ cup dry white wine
½ teaspoon dried dillweed
¼ teaspoon salt
Dash pepper
⅓ cup dairy sour cream
3 tablespoons milk
Hot cooked green noodles

Place chicken breasts between 2 pieces of clear plastic wrap. Pound out from center with meat mallet to ¼-inch thickness. Remove wrap; brush each side of chicken with melted butter or margarine. Place chicken on rack of unheated broiler pan. Broil for 6 to 8 minutes, turning once. Brush occasionally with melted butter or margarine.

Meanwhile, in small saucepan cook onion in the 1 tablespoon butter till tender but not brown. Stir in flour; add mushrooms, wine, dillweed, salt, and pepper. Cook and stir till thickened and bubbly. Cook and stir 1 minute more. Stir in sour cream and milk; heat through. Serve chicken breasts with hot noodles. Pour sauce over chicken and noodles. Makes 4 servings.

Broiler Turkey Sandwiches

¾ cup chopped cooked turkey
1 small tomato, peeled, seeded, and chopped
1 2-ounce can chopped mushrooms, drained
¼ cup dairy sour cream
2 tablespoons grated Parmesan cheese
2 tablespoons mayonnaise
1 tablespoon chopped green pepper
¼ teaspoon onion powder
⅛ teaspoon dried tarragon, crushed
2 frozen waffles, toasted

Combine all ingredients except waffles. Divide turkey mixture evenly between waffles. Place waffles on rack of unheated broiler pan. Broil for 5 to 7 minutes or till topping is bubbly. Serves 2.

Five-Spice Cornish Hen

2 tablespoons soy sauce
1 tablespoon butter
1 tablespoon honey
1 teaspoon sesame seed, toasted
⅛ teaspoon five-spice powder *or* ground ginger
1 1- to 1½-pound Cornish game hen, halved

For sauce, cook soy sauce, butter, honey, sesame seed, and five-spice powder over low heat till butter melts. Place hen halves, skin side down, on rack of unheated broiler pan. Broil for 15 to 20 minutes. Brush with sauce; turn. Broil for 10 to 15 minutes, brushing with sauce the last 5 minutes. Makes 2 servings.

Veal Rolls with Mushroom Sauce

1 small carrot
¼ pound fresh whole green beans
½ pound veal leg round steak, cut ¼ inch thick
4 slices Swiss cheese
2 tablespoons Italian salad dressing
1 tablespoon butter
2 teaspoons all-purpose flour
⅛ teaspoon dried thyme, crushed
½ cup milk
1 2½-ounce jar sliced mushrooms, drained
2 tablespoons dairy sour cream
Hot cooked rice

Cut carrot into julienne strips. In covered saucepan cook carrot and beans in a small amount of boiling salted water for 10 to 15 minutes; drain. Meanwhile, cut veal into 4 pieces. Place a cheese slice atop each piece of veal. Arrange beans and carrot strips atop cheese; roll up. Secure with wooden picks. Place rolls on rack of unheated broiler pan. Brush lightly with salad dressing. Broil for 12 to 14 minutes or till done, turning and brushing with salad dressing.

Meanwhile, for sauce melt butter. Stir in flour, thyme, and ⅛ teaspoon *salt*. Add milk. Cook and stir till thickened and bubbly. Cook and stir 1 minute more. Over low heat stir in mushrooms and sour cream. Heat through. Spoon some sauce over veal rolls before serving. Serve with rice; pass remaining sauce. Makes 2 servings.

BROILING
MAIN
DISHES

HOW TO PREPARE LAMBURGER STACK-UPS

Wrap two partially cooked bacon slices around each lamb patty. Overlap the ends of the bacon slices and fasten with wooden picks to secure. The bacon slices add a decorative touch as well as a complementary flavor to these seasoned lamburgers.

After transferring the tomato-topped broiled lamburgers to the serving platter, top each with a spoonful of the yogurt-dillweed mixture. Remind each diner to remove the wooden picks before eating his lamburger stack-up.

Lamburger Stack-Ups

8 slices bacon
1 beaten egg
¼ cup toasted wheat germ
2 tablespoons finely chopped onion
2 tablespoons chopped pimiento-stuffed olives
2 teaspoons Worcestershire sauce
¼ teaspoon garlic powder
¾ pound ground lamb
1 small tomato, thinly sliced
¼ cup plain yogurt
⅛ teaspoon dried dillweed

Partially cook the bacon; set aside. In a mixing bowl combine beaten egg, wheat germ, onion, olives, Worcestershire sauce, and garlic powder. Add ground lamb; mix well. Shape into four ½-inch-thick patties. Wrap 2 partially cooked bacon slices around each patty; fasten with wooden picks. Place patties on rack of unheated broiler pan. Broil till almost done, turning once (allow about 12 minutes total time for medium).

Place tomato slice on each patty. Broil about 1 minute longer till tomato is heated. Combine yogurt and dillweed. Remove patties to platter. Spoon about 1 tablespoon of the yogurt mixture atop each tomato slice. Makes 4 servings.

Broiler Salmon Steaks

Pictured on pages 60 and 61—

2 fresh *or* frozen salmon steaks (1 pound total)
½ of a medium sweet red pepper, thinly sliced and halved
¼ cup dry white *or* rosé wine
2 tablespoons thinly sliced green onion
2 tablespoons cooking oil
2 tablespoons lemon juice
½ teaspoon dried marjoram, crushed
¼ teaspoon dried thyme, crushed
½ of a medium avocado, seeded, peeled, and chopped

Thaw fish, if frozen. For marinade combine sliced red pepper, wine, onion, cooking oil, lemon juice, marjoram, and thyme. Place fish in plastic bag; set in shallow dish. Pour the marinade over fish. Close bag; let stand at room temperature for 2 hours, turning occasionally. (Or, marinate in refrigerator for 4 hours or overnight.) Drain, reserving the marinade.

Place fish on greased rack of unheated broiler pan. Broil till fish flakes easily when tested with fork, turning once (allow 5 minutes total for each ½ inch of thickness). Spoon on the reserved marinade the last 2 to 3 minutes of broiling time. Arrange the chopped avocado atop steaks. Garnish with lime wedges, if desired. Makes 2 servings.

Tuna Salad Melt

1 3¼-ounce can tuna
2 tablespoons chopped celery
2 tablespoons mayonnaise
1 teaspoon sweet pickle relish
¼ teaspoon onion powder
¼ teaspoon prepared mustard
2 slices rye bread, toasted
2 slices cheddar cheese

Drain and flake tuna. Combine tuna and next 5 ingredients. Spread each bread slice with half the tuna mixture. Place on rack of unheated broiler pan. Broil about 4 minutes or till topping is heated. Place cheese slices atop. Broil about 1 minute or till cheese melts. Makes 2 servings.

Herb-Cheese Fillets

½ pound fresh *or* frozen fish fillets
1 tablespoon butter, softened
2 teaspoons grated Parmesan cheese
1 teaspoon lemon juice
¼ teaspoon dried chervil, crushed
⅛ teaspoon paprika
2 teaspoons snipped parsley

Thaw fish, if frozen. Separate fillets or cut into 2 serving-size portions. Place on greased rack of unheated broiler pan. Combine next 5 ingredients; spread over fish*. Broil till fish flakes easily when tested with a fork (allow 5 minutes for each ½ inch of thickness). Top with parsley. Serves 2.

*Note: If fish is more than 1 inch thick, broil as above *except* turn when fish is half done. Add butter mixture; broil till done.

Spicy Sausage Burgers
Vegetable-Brat Kabobs
(see recipe, page 76)

Spicy Sausage Burgers

1 beaten egg
2 tablespoons water
3 tablespoons fine dry bread crumbs
¼ cup finely chopped onion
2 tablespoons chopped ripe olives
2 tablespoons grated Parmesan cheese
1 clove garlic, minced
½ pound sweet Italian sausage
½ pound ground beef
1 small onion, thinly sliced
2 tablespoons butter *or* margarine
2 French-style rolls, split and halved, *or* 4 hamburger buns, split
Pickled chili peppers (optional)

Combine beaten egg and water; stir in bread crumbs, onion, olives, Parmesan cheese, and garlic. If using link sausage, remove the meat from its casing. Add Italian sausage and ground beef to egg mixture; mix well. Shape into four ½-inch-thick patties. Place patties on rack of unheated broiler pan. Broil till well done, turning once (allow 12 to 15 minutes total time).

Meanwhile, in a small skillet cook onion slices in butter or margarine till brown. Serve burgers in French-style rolls or hamburger buns. Top each burger with some of the onion slices. If desired, garnish with pickled chili peppers. Makes 4 servings.

Potato-Topped Franks

Barbecue sauce adds a tangy touch to this fast fix-up for one —

½ **cup packaged instant**
  mashed potatoes
1 **teaspoon snipped parsley**
1 **teaspoon bottled barbecue**
  sauce
2 **frankfurters**
2 **tablespoons shredded**
  American cheese

Prepare instant mashed potatoes according to package directions. Stir together the potatoes and snipped parsley. Stir the barbecue sauce into the potato mixture to marble slightly. Keep the potato mixture warm while preparing the frankfurters. Cut the frankfurters lengthwise almost to the opposite side.

Place frankfurters, cut side up, on rack of unheated broiler pan. Broil about 2 minutes. Turn frankfurters, cut side down, and broil about 2 minutes more.

Spread the potato mixture evenly atop the frankfurters. Sprinkle the shredded American cheese atop the potato mixture on each frankfurter. Broil for 1 to 2 minutes of till cheese is melted. Makes 1 serving.

Vegetable-Brat Kabobs

Pictured on page 74 and on the cover—

4 **small boiling onions**
1 **medium yellow summer**
  squash *or* **1 medium**
  zucchini, cut into 1-inch
  chunks
¼ **cup cooking oil**
2 **tablespoons white wine**
  vinegar
½ **teaspoon garlic salt**
½ **teaspoon dried oregano,**
  crushed
¼ **teaspoon dried thyme,**
  crushed
  Dash pepper
½ **pound fully cooked**
  bratwurst, cut into
  fourths
1 **sweet red** *or* **green pepper,**
  cut into 1½-inch squares

In medium saucepan cook onions, uncovered, in boiling salted water for 10 minutes. Add squash chunks; return to boiling. Cook for 2 to 3 minutes longer; drain vegetables.

For marinade, in bowl combine oil, vinegar, garlic salt, oregano, thyme, and pepper. Add onions, squash, bratwurst, and pepper squares. Cover and marinate 6 to 8 hours or overnight in refrigerator, stirring occasionally. Drain, reserving marinade.

On four 8-inch skewers, alternately thread onions, squash, pepper pieces, and bratwurst. Place kabobs on rack of unheated broiler pan. Broil kabobs for 7 to 8 minutes; brush with a little of the reserved marinade. Turn; broil kabobs for 5 to 6 minutes longer or till brown, brushing occasionally with reserved marinade. Makes 2 servings.

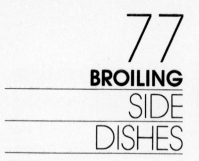

Barbecue Wheat Triangles

¼ cup whipped cream cheese
2 tablespoons cheese spread
½ teaspoon barbecue spice
4 slices whole wheat bread

Combine cream cheese, cheese spread, and barbecue spice. Spread about 1 tablespoon of the cheese mixture on 1 side of each slice of bread. Place bread slices on rack of unheated broiler pan. Broil for 2 to 3 minutes or till topping is heated through. Before serving, cut bread slices into quarters. Makes 4 servings.

Monterey Dilled Pumpernickel

½ of a 3-ounce package cream cheese, softened
¼ cup shredded Monterey Jack cheese (1 ounce)
1 tablespoon butter or margarine, softened
1 tablespoon snipped parsley
¼ teaspoon dried dillweed
4 ½-inch-thick slices pumpernickel bread

In a bowl combine cream cheese, Monterey Jack cheese, butter or margarine, parsley, and dillweed; spread cheese mixture on 1 side of each bread slice. Place slices on rack of unheated broiler pan. Broil for 3 to 4 minutes or till topping is lightly browned and heated through. Makes 4 servings.

Garlic-Herb Wedges

1 tablespoon butter or margarine, softened
¼ teaspoon Worcestershire sauce
⅛ teaspoon garlic powder
⅛ teaspoon dried basil, crushed
1 whole wheat or plain pita bread round, split horizontally

Combine butter, Worcestershire sauce, garlic powder, and basil. Spread half the herb-butter mixture on the cut side of each pita round. Cut each round into quarters. Place on rack of unheated broiler pan. Broil for 1 to 2 minutes. Serves 2.

Pesto-Topped Muffins

½ cup snipped parsley
2 tablespoons grated Parmesan cheese
2 tablespoons sliced blanched almonds
2 teaspoons dried basil, crushed
⅛ teaspoon garlic powder
3 tablespoons olive oil or cooking oil
2 English muffins or bagels, split

Place first 5 ingredients in a blender container or food processor bowl. Cover; blend with several on/off turns till a paste forms. With machine running slowly, gradually add oil; blend to the consistency of soft butter. Spread 1 tablespoon of the mixture atop each muffin half. Place halves on rack of unheated broiler pan. Broil for 1 to 2 minutes. Serves 4.

Broiler Cheesy Bagels

1 tablespoon mayonnaise *or* salad dressing
1 teaspoon snipped chives
2 bagels, split
3 tablespoons shredded Swiss cheese

In bowl combine mayonnaise or salad dressing and chives. Spread on each cut bagel half. Place bagels, cut side up, on rack of unheated broiler pan. Sprinkle bagels with the cheese. Broil for 3 to 4 minutes or till cheese melts and is lightly browned. Makes 4 servings.

Onion-Herb Frank Sticks

2 frankfurter buns
¼ cup finely chopped onion
2 tablespoons butter *or* margarine
¼ teaspoon dried marjoram, crushed
¼ teaspoon dried thyme, crushed

Split each frankfurter bun in half lengthwise. Cut each half lengthwise to make a total of 8 sticks. Cook onion in butter till tender but not brown. Stir in marjoram and thyme. Brush herb-onion butter on the 2 cut surfaces of each stick. Place sticks, buttered sides up, on rack of unheated broiler pan. Broil for 2 to 3 minutes or till golden and crispy. Makes 8 sticks.

Eggplant-Tomato Broil

4 slices eggplant, cut ½ inch thick
3 tablespoons butter *or* margarine, softened
4 thick slices tomato
2 tablespoons mayonnaise *or* salad dressing
4 teaspoons grated Parmesan cheese
⅛ teaspoon dried marjoram, crushed
Dash dried rosemary, crushed

Spread each side of eggplant slices with about 1 teaspoon of the butter or margarine. Place eggplant slices on rack of unheated broiler pan. Broil for 3 to 5 minutes on each side or till tender. Place 1 tomato slice atop each eggplant slice.

In a small bowl stir together the mayonnaise or salad dressing, grated Parmesan cheese, marjoram, and rosemary. Dollop about 2 teaspoons of the mayonnaise-cheese mixture atop each tomato slice. Broil for 1 to 2 minutes or till mayonnaise mixture is golden brown and tomatoes are heated through. If desired, sprinkle tomato slices with a little additional marjoram and rosemary. Serves 4.

Eggplant-Tomato Broil
Onion-Herb Frank Sticks

Mushrooms Stuffed with Blue Cheese

12 large fresh mushrooms
½ of a 3-ounce package cream cheese, softened
2 tablespoons crumbled blue cheese
1 tablespoon chopped pimiento

Remove stems from mushrooms; chop stems. Combine cream cheese, blue cheese, pimiento, and chopped stems. Fill mushroom crowns with cream cheese mixture. Place mushrooms on rack of unheated broiler pan. Broil about 4 minutes or till heated through. Makes 6 servings.

Cheesy Potato Slices

2 medium potatoes
2 tablespoons butter or margarine, melted
3 tablespoons grated Parmesan cheese
Dash onion powder
Dash paprika

Cut unpeeled potatoes in half crosswise; slice lengthwise into ½-inch-thick slices. Brush all sides of each potato slice with melted butter. Place potato slices on rack of unheated broiler pan. Broil for 15 to 20 minutes or till tender, turning once. Sprinkle both sides with salt. Combine cheese, onion powder, and paprika. Sprinkle evenly over potatoes. Broil about 2 minutes more. Serves 2.

Saucy Stuffed Zucchini

1 zucchini (6 to 7 inches long)
¼ cup water
1 tablespoon butter or margarine
1 small tomato, peeled, seeded, and chopped
2 tablespoons chopped mushrooms
1 tablespoon mayonnaise or salad dressing
⅛ teaspoon dried tarragon, crushed
2 tablespoons grated Romano or Parmesan cheese

Halve zucchini lengthwise. Scoop out pulp, leaving a ¼-inch shell. Chop zucchini pulp (should measure about ⅓ cup); set aside. Place zucchini shells, cut side down, in an 8-inch skillet. Add water. Cover and simmer for 5 to 6 minutes or till just tender; drain. Turn shells cut side up. Sprinkle with a little salt.

Meanwhile, in a small saucepan cook chopped zucchini pulp in butter or margarine about 3 minutes or till squash is tender. Remove from heat. Add chopped tomato, mushrooms, mayonnaise, and tarragon. Mix till the vegetables are well coated.

Spoon the vegetable mixture into zucchini shells. Place on rack of unheated broiler pan. Broil for 1 to 2 minutes. Sprinkle with the cheese. Broil 3 to 4 minutes more or till cheese browns slightly. Makes 2 servings.

Fruit Kabobs

1 ripe medium banana, cut
   into ½-inch-thick slices
Lemon juice
1 8-ounce can pineapple
   chunks
3 tablespoons currant *or*
   apple jelly
⅛ teaspoon ground cinnamon
½ of a 16-ounce can pitted
   dark sweet cherries

Brush banana slices with lemon juice. Drain pineapple, reserving 2 tablespoons liquid. Heat jelly just till melted. Stir in reserved pineapple liquid and cinnamon. On each of ten 6-inch skewers place 2 pineapple chunks, one banana slice, and 2 cherries. Brush each kabob with the jelly mixture. Place skewers on unheated broiler pan. Broil about 5 minutes, brushing once with jelly mixture again before serving. Makes 5 servings.

Pineapple Stack-Ups

4 ½-inch-thick slices canned
   brown bread *or* date-nut
   bread
1 8-ounce can pineapple
   slices, well-drained
¼ cup dairy sour cream
1 tablespoon powdered
   sugar
Dash ground coriander *or*
   ground nutmeg

Place bread slices on unheated broiler pan. Broil for 2 to 3 minutes or till lightly toasted on 1 side. Place a pineapple slice atop each bread slice. Combine sour cream and powdered sugar. Spoon about 1 tablespoon of the sour cream mixture on each pineapple slice; sprinkle with coriander. Broil for 2 to 3 minutes. Serves 4.

Lemony Blueberry Topper

4 1-inch-thick slices angel
   food cake *or* pound cake
⅓ cup frozen whipped
   dessert topping, thawed
⅓ cup lemon yogurt
1 tablespoon brown sugar
⅛ teaspoon ground nutmeg
1 cup fresh *or* frozen
   blueberries, thawed

Place cake slices on unheated broiler pan. Broil for 1 to 2 minutes or till lightly browned on 1 side. Combine dessert topping, yogurt, brown sugar, and nutmeg. Fold in blueberries. Spoon *one-fourth* of the mixture over *each* broiled cake slice. Serves 4.

Broiled Apple Slices For One

1 small apple, cored and cut
   into ½-inch-thick slices
Lemon juice
1 teaspoon maple-flavored
   syrup
Dash ground cinnamon
1 tablespoon butter *or*
   margarine, melted
Dairy sour cream
Brown sugar

Peel apple, if desired. Brush cut sides of apple slices with lemon juice. Stir syrup and cinnamon into butter. Brush slices with some of the butter mixture. Place on unheated broiler pan. Broil about 5 minutes. Turn; brush with remaining butter mixture. Broil about 3 minutes more. Transfer to serving plate. Dollop with sour cream; sprinkle with brown sugar. Serves 1.

Strawberry Cream Cheese Broil

Prepare this simple variation of a Baked Alaska when you want an elegant but easy dessert—

  ¼ **cup whipped cream cheese**
  4 **½-inch-thick slices frozen pound cake, thawed**
  1 **cup sliced fresh strawberries**
  1 **egg white**
  ⅛ **teaspoon almond extract** *or* **vanilla**
  2 **tablespoons sugar**

Spread *1 tablespoon* of the whipped cream cheese on 1 side of *each* pound cake slice. Arrange the sliced strawberries atop each cake slice to completely cover the pound cake.

For meringue, in a small bowl beat the egg white and almond extract or vanilla with a rotary beater till soft peaks form. Gradually add the sugar, about 1 tablespoon at a time, beating till the meringue forms stiff, glossy peaks and the sugar is dissolved.

Spoon about *one-fourth* of the meringue mixture atop the strawberries on *each* slice of pound cake. Place the pound cake slices on rack of unheated broiler pan. Broil for 1 to 2 minutes or till the meringue is lightly browned. Makes 4 servings.

Broiler Banana and Pineapple Dessert Cups

Banana slices hide beneath a bubbly pineapple topping—

  2 **tablespoons brown sugar**
  1 **tablespoon butter** *or* **margarine, softened**
  ¼ **cup canned crushed pineapple, drained**
  2 **tablespoons flaked coconut**
  2 **tablespoons chopped pecans**
  1 **small banana, thinly sliced**
  4 **cake dessert cups**
  2 **tablespoons chopped maraschino cherries (optional)**

In a small bowl stir together the brown sugar and butter or margarine. Stir in crushed pineapple, flaked coconut, and chopped pecans. Place *one-fourth* of the banana slices in the center of *each* cake dessert cup. Top with *one-fourth* of the pineapple mixture.

Place filled cake dessert cups on lightly greased, unheated broiler pan. Broil for 2 to 3 minutes or till pineapple mixture is bubbly and golden. Garnish with chopped maraschino cherries, if desired. Serve immediately. Serves 4.

HOW TO MAKE THE BROILER TORTE

Grease the bottom of a 7½x3½x2-inch loaf pan with shortening. Cut a piece of waxed paper or parchment paper to fit the pan bottom. Lay the piece of paper in the pan and smooth out any creases.

Turn ¼ cup batter into the paper-lined pan. Spread the batter evenly over the bottom. The batter layer will be very thin. Broil this thin layer of batter for 1½ to 2½ minutes or till lightly browned. Watch closely to prevent overbrowning.

Carefully spread another ¼ cup batter atop the lightly browned first layer. Broil as before, turning the pan for even browning if necessary. Repeat spreading with batter and broiling to make a total of eight layers.

Broiler Torte

Pictured on pages 60 and 61—

- ¼ **cup butter, softened**
- ½ **cup sugar**
- ¼ **teaspoon finely shredded orange peel**
- ½ **teaspoon almond extract**
- 3 **eggs**
- ⅓ **cup all-purpose flour**
- 3 **tablespoons cornstarch**
- ½ **cup dairy sour cream**
  Canned vanilla frosting

Beat butter with electric mixer about 30 seconds; gradually beat in ¼ *cup* of the sugar, orange peel, and ¼ *teaspoon* of the almond extract. Separate eggs. Add egg yolks, 1 at a time, beating well at high speed. Mix flour, cornstarch, and ⅛ teaspoon *salt;* stir into butter mixture. Wash beaters well. Beat egg whites with electric mixer to soft peaks. Gradually add *2 tablespoons* of the sugar, beating till stiff peaks form. Stir small amount of beaten egg whites into flour mixture. Fold flour mixture into whites. Grease and line bottom of a 7½x3½x2-inch loaf pan with parchment or waxed paper. Spread ¼ *cup* batter in pan (layer will be very thin). Broil 1½ to 2½ minutes or till lightly browned. Watch to prevent overbrowning. Carefully spread another ¼ *cup* batter atop. Broil as above; turn pan if needed to brown evenly. Repeat layering and broiling, making 8 layers total. Combine sour cream, remaining 2 tablespoons sugar, and remaining ¼ teaspoon extract. Spread over cake. Broil 1 to 2 minutes. Cool 10 minutes. Loosen sides; cool 10 minutes. Invert onto waxed-paper-lined tray. Remove parchment paper. Invert onto plate; remove waxed paper. Frost cake. If desired, garnish with mandarin orange sections and sliced almonds. Chill till serving time. Serves 8.

MENUS

The toaster oven is ideal for dinners for only one or two. It avoids heating up your large oven and the kitchen. Each menu features toaster oven specialties plus additional recipes to round out the meal. Along with everyday fare, there are distinctive recipes such as the *Citrus-Spinach Salad, Veal Rolls with Romano Sauce,* and *Individual Cheesecakes* pictured here (see recipes, page 86).

MENU
DRESSED-UP DINNER FOR TWO

**Veal Roll-Ups with Romano Sauce
Citrus-Spinach Salad
French bread
Individual Cheesecakes
Beverage**

Pictured on pages 84 and 85—

Citrus-Spinach Salad

**1½ cups torn spinach *or* Boston lettuce, *or* iceberg lettuce
1 large orange, peeled and sectioned *or* cut up
1 tablespoon salad oil
1 tablespoon vinegar *or* wine vinegar
¼ teaspoon sugar
⅛ teaspoon dried mint, crushed
Cashews (optional)**

Place torn spinach or lettuce in a medium bowl. Add orange sections. Toss lightly; cover and chill. In a small bowl combine the salad oil, vinegar, sugar, and mint. Stir together till well blended. Cover and chill. Stir together again and pour over the lettuce-fruit mixture. Toss salad lightly to coat. Garnish with cashews, if desired. Serve immediately. Makes 2 servings.

Veal Roll-Ups with Romano Sauce

**1 10-ounce package frozen asparagus spears *or* frozen broccoli spears
4 veal cutlets *or* ½ pound veal leg steak, cut ¼ inch thick
1 tablespoon butter or margarine
1 teaspoon all-purpose flour
¼ teaspoon instant beef bouillon granules
Dash white pepper
¾ cup milk *or* light cream
2 tablespoons grated Romano or grated Parmesan cheese
⅛ teaspoon dried chervil, crushed**

In a medium saucepan cook asparagus or broccoli spears, covered, in a small amount of boiling salted water for 3 to 5 minutes or till crisp-tender; drain. Cut veal steak into 4 portions. Sprinkle meat with salt and pepper. Arrange asparagus spears on meat; roll up. Secure with wooden picks. Place on rack of unheated broiler pan. Broil 12 to 14 minutes for medium doneness, turning once. Remove wooden picks.

Meanwhile, prepare sauce. In a small saucepan melt the butter or margarine; stir in the flour, bouillon granules, and white pepper. Add milk or cream all at once; cook and stir over medium heat till mixture is thickened and bubbly. Cook and stir 1 minute more. Stir in the Romano or Parmesan cheese and chervil; heat through. Place roll-ups on serving platter; spoon some of the sauce over. Pass remaining sauce. Makes 2 servings.

Individual Cheesecakes

Pictured on the cover and page 84—

**2 ¼- to ½-inch slices of a 17-ounce roll refrigerated sugar cookie dough
1 4-ounce container whipped cream cheese
3 tablespoons sugar
1 tablespoon milk
½ teaspoon vanilla
1 egg
2 tablespoons strawberry, raspberry, apricot, *or* peach preserves
Chopped walnuts *or* almonds (optional)**

Press cookie dough slices evenly over bottoms of two ½-cup soufflé dishes or 6-ounce custard cups. Bake in a 350° oven for 8 to 10 minutes or till golden. In a small mixer bowl beat cream cheese about 30 seconds or till smooth. Add sugar, milk, and vanilla; beat well. Add egg; beat just till blended (do not overbeat).

Pour over cookie crust in soufflé dishes. Bake in a 350° oven about 20 minutes or till center appears set. Cool, then chill at least 2 hours or till serving time. To serve, spread 1 tablespoon preserves over each cheesecake; sprinkle with chopped nuts if desired. Makes 2 servings.

MENU
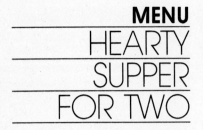

**Bacon 'n' Beef Loaves
Baked Peas Deluxe
Crispy Fried Noodles
Fresh fruit and cheese
Beverage**

Bacon 'n' Beef Loaves

**1 beaten egg
1 tablespoon milk
3 tablespoons fine dry bread crumbs
1 2-ounce can chopped mushrooms, drained
1 tablespoon finely chopped onion
¼ teaspoon garlic salt
Dash pepper
½ pound ground beef
2 slices bacon, halved crosswise**

In mixing bowl combine beaten egg, milk, bread crumbs, mushrooms, onion, garlic salt, and pepper. Add ground beef; mix well. Shape into two 4-inch-long loaves. Place 2 bacon slice halves over each loaf to form a crisscross design on the top of the loaf.

Place loaves on rack of unheated broiler pan so meat does not bake in drippings. Bake in a 350° oven about 50 minutes or till done. Makes 2 servings.

Menu Tip: Take advantage of staggered cooking times to dovetail meal preparations and cleanup. While the meat loaves are baking the first twenty minutes, set the table and toss together the easy vegetable dish. After you put the peas in the oven with the main dish, start cooking the noodles and take a few moments to tidy up the kitchen before serving dinner.

Baked Peas Deluxe

**1 8½-ounce can peas, drained, or one 8-ounce can cut green beans, drained
1 tablespoon finely chopped celery
1 tablespoon French salad dressing**

In a 10-ounce casserole or custard cup combine the peas, chopped celery, salad dressing, dash *salt,* and dash *pepper.* Bake, covered, in a 350° oven 25 to 30 minutes or till peas are heated through. Makes 2 servings.

Crispy Fried Noodles

**1 cup medium noodles
2 tablespoons butter *or* margarine
3 tablespoons sliced green onion
¼ teaspoon dried basil, crushed (optional)**

Cook noodles according to package directions; drain. Rinse in cold water; drain well. Preheat a large skillet over medium-high heat; add butter or margarine. Stir-fry green onion in hot butter for 1 minute; add noodles and basil. Stir-fry for 7 to 10 minutes or till just beginning to brown. Serve warm. Makes 2 servings.

MENU
INDOOR PICNIC FOR TWO

Broiled Brats
Potato Salad
Chocolate Malt Bars
Beverage

Broiled Brats

2 frankfurter buns
2 fully cooked bratwurst links
½ cup cranberry-apple drink
1 teaspoon cornstarch
⅛ teaspoon ground nutmeg
½ cup sauerkraut, rinsed and drained
1 tablespoon finely chopped onion

Open buns; do not break apart. Place, cut side up, on unheated rack of broiler pan. Broil till toasted; remove. Place bratwursts on rack. Broil about 8 minutes, turning once. Meanwhile, in a small saucepan stir apple drink into cornstarch and nutmeg; add sauerkraut and onion. Cook and stir till thickened and bubbly; cook and stir 2 minutes more. Serve bratwursts on buns; spoon sauerkraut mixture atop. Makes 2 servings.

Potato Salad

1½ cups frozen loose-pack hash brown potatoes
2 tablespoons thinly sliced radishes
1 tablespoon thinly sliced green onion
2 tablespoons mayonnaise
2 tablespoons plain yogurt
1 teaspoon prepared mustard
¼ teaspoon celery seed
1 hard-cooked egg, coarsely chopped

Cook potatoes in enough boiling salted water to cover, for 3 to 5 minutes or till almost tender; drain. Combine potatoes, radishes, and onion. Stir together the next 4 ingredients, ½ teaspoon *salt,* and dash *pepper.* Add to potato mixture; toss lightly to coat. Fold in the egg. Cover; chill thoroughly. Makes 2 servings.

Chocolate Malt Bars

3 tablespoons butter *or* margarine
⅓ cup sugar
1 egg
1 5½-ounce can (½ cup) chocolate-flavored syrup
½ cup all-purpose flour
3 tablespoons chocolate-flavored instant malted milk powder
¼ cup chopped walnuts
¼ cup chocolate-flavored instant malted milk powder
2 tablespoons butter *or* margarine, softened
¾ cup sifted powdered sugar
1 to 2 tablespoons milk

Grease an 8x6½x2-inch baking dish; set aside. In a small mixer bowl beat 3 tablespoons butter or margarine for 30 seconds. Add sugar and beat till fluffy. Add egg; beat well. Stir in chocolate-flavored syrup, then flour and 3 tablespoons malted milk powder. (Batter will look curdled.) Fold in chopped walnuts. Spread batter in prepared baking dish. Bake in a 350° oven for 30 to 35 minutes or till done. Cool on a wire rack.

For frosting beat together ¼ cup malted milk powder and 2 tablespoons butter or margarine. Slowly beat in the sifted powdered sugar and enough milk to make of spreading consistency. Frost and cut into bars. Makes 8 bars.

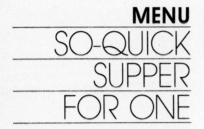

MENU
SO-QUICK SUPPER FOR ONE

**Cheesy Frank Roll-Ups
Easy Baked Corn
Frozen Peach Tart
Beverage**

Easy Baked Corn

**½ of an 8½-ounce can (½ cup) cream-style corn
1 tablespoon chopped green pepper
1 tablespoon finely chopped pimiento
½ teaspoon minced dried onion
Dash celery seed
1 tablespoon herb-seasoned stuffing croutons**

Combine corn, green pepper, pimiento, minced onion, and celery seed. Turn into a 6-ounce custard cup. Bake in a 375° oven about 20 minutes or till heated through. Sprinkle with croutons. Bake about 5 minutes more. Makes 1 serving.

Frozen Peach Tart

**2 tablespoons peach yogurt
2 tablespoons frozen whipped dessert topping, thawed
¼ cup canned diced peaches, well drained
1 teaspoon orange marmalade
1 graham cracker tart shell**

For filling, combine yogurt, dessert topping, peaches, and marmalade. Stir till well blended. Turn into tart shell. Freeze till firm. Remove from freezer 10 minutes before serving. Makes 1 serving.

Cheesy Frank Roll-Ups

Prepare the corn dish during the first 10 minutes while these roll-ups are cooking—

**¼ cup cream-style cottage cheese
1 tablespoon sweet pickle relish
½ teaspoon prepared mustard
2 frankfurters
2 6-inch flour tortillas
¼ cup shredded American cheese
Thinly sliced green onion**

In a small bowl combine the cream-style cottage cheese, pickle relish, and prepared mustard. Slice frankfurters lengthwise, cutting to *but not through* opposite side. Stuff each frankfurter with half the cottage cheese mixture.

Place a stuffed frankfurter, stuffing side down, atop a tortilla. Fold tortilla so opposite edges overlap atop frankfurter. Repeat with remaining frankfurter and tortilla. Place tortillas, seam side down, in a shallow casserole.

Bake, covered, in a 375° oven for 30 minutes. Uncover and sprinkle with the shredded American cheese. Return to oven and bake about 5 minutes more. Sprinkle with thinly sliced green onion before serving. Makes 1 serving.

MENU
EASY OVEN DINNER FOR ONE

Italian Chicken
Glazed Onion Wedges
Fruit Salad
Hard rolls
Choco-Orange Parfait
(see Menu Tip)
Beverage

Italian Chicken

While the chicken and onions bake, prepare the salad and dessert—

2 tablespoons catsup
1 tablespoon vinegar
¼ teaspoon dried oregano, crushed
⅛ teaspoon dried rosemary, crushed
1 chicken drumstick with thigh attached

For sauce, in a small bowl combine catsup, vinegar, oregano, and rosemary. Place chicken on rack of unheated broiler pan so chicken does not bake in drippings; spoon sauce over. Bake, uncovered, in a 350° oven about 45 minutes or till chicken is done. Makes 1 serving.

Glazed Onion Wedges

1 small onion, cut into small wedges
1 tablespoon finely chopped celery
1 teaspoon brown sugar
⅛ teaspoon dried basil, crushed
  Butter or margarine
1 tablespoon grated Parmesan cheese

Place onion wedges and celery in an individual baking dish; sprinkle with brown sugar and basil. Dot with butter or margarine. Bake, covered, in a 350° oven about 45 minutes or till onion is tender. Sprinkle with Parmesan cheese. Bake, uncovered, about 5 minutes longer or till cheese is lightly browned. Makes 1 serving.

Fruit Salad

2 tablespoons dairy sour cream
2 teaspoons lemon or lime juice
2 teaspoons honey
  Dash ground cinnamon
1 small peach, peeled, pitted, and sliced, or ½ of an 8-ounce can peach slices, drained
¼ cup blueberries and/or red raspberries

For dressing, combine the sour cream, lemon or lime juice, honey, and cinnamon. Arrange peach slices and blueberries in a sherbet dish or icer or on lettuce-lined salad plate. Spoon dressing over fruit. Makes 1 serving.

Menu Tip: Dress up a dinner for one with an easy but elegant dessert like Choco-Orange Parfait. Layer orange sherbet with crushed chocolate cookies or substitute your favorite sherbet and any leftover cookies. If you don't have parfait glasses, use a fancy water goblet or wineglass.

Prepare the parfait after you put the chicken and onion wedges in to bake and freeze till serving time. It'll be a cool and frosty refresher come dessert.

Glazed Onion Wedges
Italian Chicken
Fruit Salad
Choco-Orange Parfait

MENU
SEAFOOD SUPPER FOR TWO

Baked Scallops in Foil
Zucchini-Tomato
Combo
Apple Wedges with
Poppy-Seed Dressing
Crescent rolls
Mocha Sundaes
(see Menu Tip)
Beverage

Baked Scallops in Foil

- ½ **pound fresh *or* frozen scallops**
- 1 **tablespoon butter *or* margarine, melted**
- 1 **tablespoon finely snipped chives**
- 2 **tablespoons dry sherry**

Thaw scallops, if frozen. Cut any large scallops in half. Place *half* of the scallops on a 12x12-inch piece of foil. Turn up edges of foil. Drizzle scallops with *half* of the butter or margarine. Sprinkle *half* of the chives over the scallops. Pour *1 tablespoon* of the sherry over the scallops. Bring opposite sides of foil together and fold twice to seal; seal ends. Repeat with remaining scallops and other ingredients on another square of foil. Bake foil packets in a 375° oven for 15 to 20 minutes or till scallops are cooked. Makes 2 servings.

Menu Tip: *Mocha Sundaes* can be as plain or fancy as you please. Drizzle chocolate-flavored syrup over scoops of coffee ice cream to make an easy, light ending to this tasty dinner. Or let your imagination run wild. Dip scoops of coffee ice cream and roll in chopped nuts or coconut. Place balls in sherbet glasses in freezer till serving time. Drizzle lightly with coffee liqueur or crème de cacao.

Zucchini-Tomato Combo

Cook the zucchini while you're getting the scallop packets ready for the oven—

- ½ **cup sliced zucchini**
- 1 **small tomato, peeled, seeded, and chopped (½ cup)**
- ½ **teaspoon dried parsley flakes**
- ½ **teaspoon lemon juice**
- ⅛ **teaspoon celery salt**

Cook zucchini, covered, in boiling salted water for 5 minutes; drain well. Combine with remaining ingredients and dash *pepper* in 1 cup casserole. Bake, covered, in a 375° oven for 15 to 20 minutes. Serves 2.

Apple Wedges with Poppy-Seed Dressing

- 2 **tablespoons orange juice**
- 2 **teaspoons salad oil**
- 1 **teaspoon honey**
- ⅛ **teaspoon poppy seed**
  Dash salt
- 1 **medium apple**
  Lettuce leaves

For dressing, in a small bowl combine the orange juice, salad oil, honey, poppy seed, and salt. Stir together till well blended. Cover and chill till serving time. Core apple and cut into wedges. Place on 2 individual lettuce-lined salad plates. Stir chilled dressing and spoon over apple wedges. Makes 2 servings.

INDEX